Praise for Terry
Air Mail

D1150681

'Terry Ravenscroft has end~~~~ ~~~~~.., ~~ ~~~ nanus of the airlines. And now the airlines have endured Terry. Very funny.'
Griff Rhys Jones

'Anyone taking a flight this year must take a copy of *Air Mail* with them. Hilarious.'
June Whitfield

'Sure to have you rolling in the aisles.'
Sunday Times Travel Magazine

'An absolute must for anyone who has travelled by plane and been annoyed. A wickedly funny book.'
Rory McGrath

'Terry Ravenscroft's *Air Mail* is terrific.'
Roy Hudd

'Devilishly funny. Terry Ravenscroft is the comic correspondent from hell.'
Andy Hamilton

'Terry Ravenscroft was a very funny scriptwriter. He's now a very funny letter writer too.'
Barry Cryer

About the Author

The day after Terry Ravenscroft threw in his mundane factory job to become a TV scriptwriter, he was involved in a car accident that left him unable to turn his head. Since then, he has never looked back. Before they took him away, he wrote scripts for Les Dawson, *The Two Ronnies*, Morecambe and Wise, *Alas Smith and Jones*, *Not The Nine O'Clock News*, Dave Allen, Frankie Howerd, Ken Dodd, Roy Hudd, Hale and Pace, and quite a few others. He also wrote many episodes of the situation comedy *Terry and June*, and the award-winning BBC Radio series *Star Terk Two*.

His other books include the bestselling *Air Mail* (2007) – another collection of comic correspondence from the inimitable T Ravenscroft (Mr) – and the novel *Football Crazy* (2006).

He has his own website at www.topcomedy.co.uk.

Dear Customer Services

Letters From the World's Most Troublesome Shopper

Terry Ravenscroft

Michael O'Mara Books Limited

First published in 2008 by
Michael O'Mara Books Limited
9 Lion Yard
Tremadoc Road
London SW4 7NQ

A CIP catalogue record for this book is available from the British Library.

Papers used by Michael O'Mara Books Limited are natural, recyclable
products made from wood grown in sustainable forests. The manufacturing
processes conform to the environmental regulations of the country of origin.

ISBN: 978-1-84317-296-3

1 3 5 7 9 10 8 6 4 2

Designed by Burville-Riley Partnership

Printed in Great Britain by CPI Cox & Wyman, Reading, Berks

www.mombooks.com

Warning to Those of a Non-Humorous Disposition

This book is intended as a humorous work and such 'accusations' as there are (whether stated expressly or by implication) against the companies featured in this book should not be taken seriously or indeed literally.

The author wishes to thank the companies for their goodwill, enduring patience and their much appreciated contribution to this work.

The Elms
Wenter Road
New Mills
High Peak
Derbyshire

Ferrero Ltd
Rickmansworth   10th April
Herts
WD3 10CB

Dear Ferrero

On the recommendation of a friend, I recently purchased a jar
of your Nutella Hazelnut Chocolate Spread. It was quite tasty,
but despite going through it with a fine toothcomb I could
find no trace of any hazelnuts whatsoever. Is it possible I got
a faulty jar?

Yours faithfully

T Ravenscroft (Mr)

FERRERO UK LIMITED

Head Office: Batchworth Heath House, Batchworth Heath, Rickmansworth, Herts. WD3 1QB

15 April

Mr T Ravenscroft
The Elms
Wenter Road
New Mills
High Peak
Derbyshire

Dear Mr Ravenscroft

Thank you for your recent letter regarding hazelnuts in Nutella.

In the production process for Nutella there are rollers that grind the paste until it is smooth. That is why you cannot feel the nuts.

Thank you for writing and I now enclose a jar which I hope you will enjoy.

Yours sincerely

Karen Davies
Consumer Relations Department

Registered in England. Registration No. 876127
Directors: M. Caretto (Managing Director) M. L. G. Dillon M. Galli S. Torcelli

Karen Davies
Ferrero UK Ltd
Batchworth Heath House
Batchworth Heath
Rickmansworth
Herts
WD3 1QB

The Elms
Wenter Road
New Mills
High Peak
Derbyshire

18th April

Dear Karen Davies

Thank you for your letter of 15th April and the jar of Nutella. Yes, I am sure I will enjoy it – the quality of Nutella was never in any doubt, it was just that as your label said 'Hazelnut Chocolate Spread', I not unreasonably expected something with nuts in it. Maybe you should consider making your label a little clearer in this regard?

Now I have some good news for you! I believe you may have accidentally stumbled on a really exciting new advertising slogan for your product. It is contained in the last sentence of your letter. I refer of course to your phrase 'You cannot feel the nuts!' (The exclamation mark is mine.) It definitely has a ring to it, that certain *je ne sais quoi* all great advertising slogans have, a sort of cross between 'You can't tell Stork from butter' and 'Nuts, whole hazelnuts, Cadburys make 'em and they cover them with chocolate'. If you were to use this slogan in a television commercial, I am quite sure the sales of Nutella would hit the roof. Comedy is used to great effect in commercials these days, so might I suggest the following?

SCENE: A SULTAN'S HAREM.

A EUNUCH IS SPOONING NUTELLA INTO HIS MOUTH DIRECTLY FROM THE JAR, WITH OBVIOUS ENJOYMENT. ONE OF THE SULTAN'S WIVES, SCANTILY DRESSED IN BRA AND

DIAPHANOUS PANTALOONS, IS FONDLING THE EUNUCH IN THE GROIN AREA OF HIS TROUSERS.

THEY BOTH TURN TO THE CAMERA IN UNISON AND SAY: – 'You cannot feel the nuts!'

Or is that a bit too saucy? I look forward to hearing from you with your comments.

Yours faithfully

T Ravenscroft (Mr)

FERRERO UK LIMITED

Head Office: Batchworth Heath House, Batchworth Heath, Rickmansworth, Herts. WD3 1QB

21 April

Mr T Ravenscroft
The Elms
Wenter Road
New Mills
High Peak
Derbyshire

Dear Mr Ravenscroft

Thank you for your second letter regarding Nutella.

I will pass your suggestion for the new Nutella advertisement
on to my colleagues in the Marketing Department.

Once again, thank you for taking the time and trouble
to write.

Yours sincerely

Karen Davies
Consumer Relations Department

Registered in England. Registration No. 876127
Directors: M. Caretto (Managing Director) M. L. G. Dillon M. Galli S. Torcelli

The Elms
Wenter Road
New Mills
High Peak
Derbyshire

Ena Baxter
Baxters of Speyside Ltd
Fochabers
Moray
Scotland
IV32 7LD

18th March

Dear Ena Baxter

I have been buying your Cock-a-Leekie soup for many years, and an absolutely splendid soup it is too. It is then with no small regret that I must now make a complaint about it; for on opening my most recent can, taste buds at the ready and appetite fully whetted, I was surprised to discover that the contents of the can were 90 per cent rice. Now, I like rice as much as the next man – as long as the next man isn't a Chinaman, of course – but 90 per cent is a bit too much rice even for a man who likes rice.

There is no doubt a fault with your rice dispenser and you would do well to have it checked out. Fortunately, I had another can of Cock-a-Leekie in the cupboard, and I am happy to report that on opening it I found it to be well up to Baxters' usual excellent standard.

I am sure that being Scottish you will be glad to learn that the original faulty can wasn't wasted. Parsimony as well as necessity being the mother of invention, I drained off what little liquid there was, added milk and sugar to taste, and had it as a rice pudding for afters. And very nice it was too, the slight chicken flavour of the rice adding a little extra interest to what can sometimes be a rather dull pudding. In fact, thinking about it, if you ever feel the urge to add puddings to your catalogue of culinary goodies, you could do a lot worse than market it yourselves. Maybe you could call it 'Cock-of-Puddings'?

Yours faithfully

T Ravenscroft (Mr)

BY APPOINTMENT
TO H.M QUEEN ELIZABETH II
FRUIT CANNERS
W. A. BAXTER & SONS LTD.
FOCHABERS, SCOTLAND

Baxters

Baxters of Speyside Limited
Fochabers Scotland IV32 7LD

24 March
Reference: 20517

Mr T Ravenscroft
The Elms
Wenter Road
New Mills
High Peak
Derbyshire

Dear Mr Ravenscroft,

Thank you for your letter of 18 March, to which Mrs Ena Baxter has asked me to give my immediate, personal attention. May I first of all say how concerned we are to learn of your disappointment with our Cock-a-Leekie Soup which you purchased recently.

We are always pleased to hear from customers how much they enjoy our products and we are consequently all the more concerned that you have purchased one which does not come up to the high standard you have come to expect.

We make our soup in huge kettles, much larger than the original Mrs Baxter ever used, and although the mix is heated up to boiling point, the vegetables are not actually "cooked" until they are sealed in a can. We do notice that, even with the huge stirrers we use, the bottom of the kettle can be thicker than the top. As we are aware of this, we take the first and the last few cans off to ensure that our discerning consumers only have the traditional Cock-a-Leekie Soup normally associated with Baxters. It would appear in this instance that you have purchased one of the cans which should have been removed. You may be sure, however, that your complaint will be the subject of investigation with our Production Manager. In order to assist us with our investigation I would be grateful if you could return to us the coded end of the can concerned, if this is still available; unfortunately the bar code on the label does not give us the information we require. I enclose a prepaid envelope for this purpose.

Please be assured that my colleagues and I try very hard to ensure that we maintain the high quality standards of all our food products. For instance, I would mention that we sample every delivery of ingredients and packaging material on arrival at the factory. All the meats, vegetables and fruits we use are prepared, washed, trimmed then inspected, either on site or at our suppliers, before progressing to the kitchen. We take great care to ensure that our suppliers match our high standards. This involves frequent visits by our trained Technical Staff both within the UK and abroad.

During production a Quality Control Inspector is permanently stationed at each stage to supervise the processing operations; among the particular duties of the Inspector in the Soup Department is testing every individual batch before it is filled. Samples are subsequently tested and examined throughout the day by our Analytical and Microbiological Laboratory staff and further tasted four times daily by a Management Panel.

Please accept my sincere apologies for the inconvenience you have been caused, but I trust that the above explanation restores your confidence in our company and its products. I thank you for the time you have taken to draw our attention to this very unusual complaint, as it is only with feedback such as this that we can improve on our already strict attention to detail.

As a gesture of our goodwill, I have pleasure in enclosing some vouchers which will enable you to obtain replacement Baxter products from your local store. I hope you will accept these with our compliments and that you enjoy the products you choose. Also enclosed is some information about our Visitors Centre which I hope you will find of interest.

Assuring you of our best attention at all times.

Yours sincerely,

Miss M Macpherson
Quality Audit Manager

Your ref 20517

The Elms
Wenter Road
New Mills
High Peak
Derbyshire

1st April

Miss M Macpherson
Quality Audit Manager
Baxters of Speyside Ltd
Fochabers
Scotland
IV32 7LD

Dear Miss Macpherson

Thank you for your prompt and informative reply, and for the gift vouchers, which I passed on to the needy. However, your letter leaves me confused to say the least. You write that you make your soup in huge kettles, 'much larger than the original Mrs Baxter ever used', yet your television advertisement clearly shows Ena Baxter making the soup in her kitchen using ordinary utensils. Perhaps you can clear this up for me?

I look forward to your reply.

Yours sincerely

T Ravenscroft (Mr)

PS. Since my initial letter to you, I have become a real fan of Cock-a-Leekie-flavoured rice pudding. If you'd like to try it, I've found that 85 per cent Ambrosia Creamed Rice to 15 per cent Cock-a-Leekie Soup gives the best results. If you were to market this as Cock-of-Puddings, I am quite sure you would have a winner on your hands.

Baxters

Baxters of Speyside Limited
Fochabers Scotland IV32 7LD

9 April
Reference: 20517

Mr T Ravenscroft
The Elms
Wenter Road
New Mills
High Peak
Derbyshire

Dear Mr Ravenscroft,

Thank you for your letter of 1 April, further to your complaint about a can
of our Cock-a-Leekie Soup.

The television advert depicting Mrs Baxter shows her developing recipes
in her kitchen. These recipes are then transferred into the factory where
we indeed use huge kettles in the preparation of over 50 million cans of
soup per year.

I hope this satisfactorily answers your enquiry and that we can continue
to count on your valued custom.

Assuring you of our best attention at all times.

Yours sincerely,

Miss M Macpherson
Quality Audit Manager

The Elms
Wenter Road
New Mills
Your ref 20517   High Peak
Derbyshire

Miss M Macpherson
Quality Audit Manager   11th April
Baxters of Speyside Ltd
Fochabers
Scotland
IV32 7LD

Dear Miss Macpherson

You can always count on my valued custom. I have been enjoying your soups ever since I can remember, and the fact that you choose to mislead the general public with your television commercial won't stop me now.

You didn't mention whether or not you might have any interest in my idea for 'Cock-of-Puddings'. Since I last wrote to you, I have improved it with the addition of a little nutmeg and a hint of honey, and it really is quite something now, even if I say so myself. I had friends round for dinner the other evening and served it up as dessert with a spoonful of Robertson's Raspberry Jam, and everyone present voted it an unqualified success. Indeed, Laura Barker remarked that it was 'to die for'.

I will be visiting Scotland next month with my wife and family. Whilst we are there, I would very much like to visit your factory and tour your Visitor Centre, regardless of whether you go for my 'Cock-of-Puddings' idea or not. Do I need to book in advance or can I just turn up on the day?

My kindest regards to you.

Yours sincerely

T Ravenscroft (Mr)

BY APPOINTMENT
TO H.M. QUEEN ELIZABETH II
FRUIT CANNERS
W. A. BAXTER & SONS LTD.
FOCHABERS, SCOTLAND

Baxters

Baxters of Speyside Limited
Fochabers Scotland IV32 7LD

22 April
Reference: 20517

Mr T Ravenscroft
The Elms
Wenter Road
New Mills
High Peak
Derbyshire

Dear Mr Ravenscroft,

Thank you for your recent letter, further to your original complaint about a can of our Cock-a-Leekie Soup.

We do not make desserts and hence my not picking up on your "Cock of Pudding" suggestion.

Our Visitors Centre is open to the public, in fact we had 205,000 visitors last year. There is no need to book, but if you want to see the factory in operation I would suggest you plan to be here between 10 and 11 in the morning, or 2 and 4 in the afternoon. We have an excellent restaurant which may help to round out your visit. The factory closes early on a Friday afternoon and, of course, does not operate at the weekends nor during the planned holidays which are 23 June to 4 July inclusive and 11 to 15 August inclusive.

Assuring you of our best attention at all times.

Yours sincerely,

Miss M Macpherson
Quality Audit Manager

Your ref 20517

The Elms
Wenter Road
New Mills
High Peak
Derbyshire

Miss M Macpherson
Quality Audit Manager
Baxters of Speyside Ltd
Fochabers
Scotland
IV32 7LD

25th April

Dear Miss Macpherson

I was sorry to learn that you don't make desserts, but then at one time you didn't make soups, did you, so I'm quite sure you will change your mind once you've tasted Cock-of-Puddings, a sample of which I enclose. This is the definitive version, and consists of 4 parts of Ambrosia Creamed Rice to 1 part of Baxters Cock-a-Leekie Soup, half a teaspoon of honey, quarter of a teaspoon of minced root ginger, and a little nutmeg. Utter bliss!

I haven't got canning facilities of course, but the old salmon tin I have put it in has been thoroughly sterilised in Milton, before re-sealing the tin lid with superglue, so you have nothing to fear on the health front.

My family and I plan to visit your Visitors Centre on the 23rd of May, and your factory the following day, all being well. By then you and Ena Baxter will have had the chance to sample Cock-of-Puddings and evaluate it. Indeed, I will be very surprised if you're not producing it in vast quantities in one of your huge kettles by then. Whereabouts is your office? I'll drop in on you.

Incidentally, the expression 'to die for', which I told you was used by Laura Barker to describe Cock-of-Puddings, proved to be a little unfortunate, as two days later she dropped dead. But I'm quite sure it had nothing to do with the pudding.

My regards to you.

Yours sincerely

T Ravenscroft (Mr)

Baxters

Baxters of Speyside Limited
Fochabers Scotland IV32 7LD

5 May
Reference: 20517

Mr T Ravenscroft
The Elms
Wenter Road
New Mills
High Peak
Derbyshire

Dear Mr Ravenscroft,

Thank you for your most recent letter about your Cock of Puddings. The sample which you kindly returned to us had deteriorated in the post and I am sure you would appreciate our reluctance to taste it.

Finally, I do hope you enjoy your visit to the factory in May. Unfortunately I will be away on holiday in the USA that week, but I am sure that the Visitor Centre staff will ensure your visit is most enjoyable.

Assuring you of our best attention at all times.

Yours sincerely,

Miss M Macpherson
Quality Audit Manager

The Elms
Wenter Road
New Mills
High Peak
Derbyshire

Your ref 20517

Miss M Macpherson
Quality Audit Manager
Baxters of Speyside Ltd
Fochabers
Scotland
IV32 7LD

11th May

Dear Miss Macpherson

Coward.

Yours sincerely

T Ravenscroft (Mr)

The Elms
Wenter Road
New Mills
High Peak
Derbyshire

McVitie's
The Vegetable Kitchen   19th March
Admail 827
Fakenham
Norfolk
NR21 0FF

Dear McVitie's

I'm afraid that I have a rather serious complaint to make about one of your vegetarian products. Yesterday I purchased a packet of your Linda McCartney Deep Country Pies from my local supermarket, and later heated them up for supper along with some oven chips, for my three children and myself. I have to report that in at least one of the pies, the pie eaten by me, was a quantity of meat. It is difficult to believe that with a pie whose ingredients already include water, wheatflour, vegetable oil, onion, rehydrated soya protein concentrate, vegetarian seasoning, modified starch, wheat protein, soya flour, salt, malt extract and sodium there would be any room left in it for meat, but meat in it there was. There could very well have been meat in the other three pies as well, but unfortunately my children had eaten them before I had the chance to check. (The speed with which my children dispatched the pies would suggest that they did indeed contain meat, since they are reluctant vegetarians at best, and anything put before them with meat in it tends to go down their throats without touching the sides.)

Needless to say, I am very disappointed in your 'vegetarian' pies and certainly won't be buying any more. I would like your comments on this as I may decide to take the matter further with the appropriate authorities.

Yours faithfully

T Ravenscroft (Mr)

ROSS HOUSE, GRIMSBY DN31 3SW.

Our Ref: CW0064

8 April

Mr T Ravenscroft
The Elms
Wenter Road
New Mills
High Peak
Derbyshire

Dear Mr Ravenscroft,

I write further to your letter dated the 19 March, regarding your complaint of a recent purchase of our Linda McCartney Deep Country Pies, which you believe contained meat. On behalf of the Company I would like to apologise for the upset and the inconvenience that you have been caused.

I would like to assure you that the products in our range are produced in a factory in Norfolk, which is totally dedicated to the Linda McCartney range and no other products are made there. The factory is totally meat free and the staff canteen is also totally vegetarian as no meat is allowed on site. This new factory took in a number of environmentally friendly issues during building, e.g., uses ozone-friendly ammonia refrigerants, catalytic converters and natural gas.

A number of our products including the Deep Country Pies contain Textured Vegetable Protein, which not only looks like meat, but also has a similar taste. This is a meat substitute, ideal for vegetarians, who, whilst liking the taste and texture of meat, are against the slaughter of animals.

The factory Technical Manager at the production unit concerned has assured me that controls within the factory are very strict and the staff are fully aware on the handling of vegetarian products.

I hope I have allayed your fears, as all of our vegetarian customers are very important to us. It would also be useful to know if there is any remaining product available so that we can have it analysed to help put your mind at ease.

Once again I would like to thank you for the time and trouble you have taken to contact us about your complaint and I look forward to hearing from you, a stamped addressed envelope is enclosed for your convenience.

Assuring you of our best attention at all times.

Yours sincerely

Mrs Angie Wilding
Customer Care Department

The Elms
Wenter Road
New Mills
High Peak
Derbyshire

Your ref CW0064

Angie Wilding   10th April
McVitie's Prepared Foods
Ross House
Grimsby
DN31 3SW

Dear Angie Wilding

Thank you for your very informative letter of 8th April. Having read it, I feel that I could almost start up a vegetarian products factory myself! You are to be congratulated on making textured vegetable protein both resemble and taste like meat. It would fool Desperate Dan himself. It certainly fooled me!

On reflection, I think I may have been guilty of prejudging your Linda McCartney Deep Country Pies. Before I became a veggie, I was convinced that most people benefited from a bit of meat inside them now and again, but I am now convinced that your pies are a more than adequate substitute.

Since my original letter, I have tried some more of your range, and I must say I was most impressed, as was my family. It is my hope to get my family completely vegetarian this year, including our pets, and your excellent range of products can only help me to achieve this ambition. Our canary is already vegetarian of course, but our dog Rantzen still insists on bits of Chum mixed in with his dog biscuits. Are your Deep Country Pies fit for dogs? If so, I could try mixing bits of them in instead.

I look forward to hearing from you.

Yours sincerely

T Ravenscroft (Mr)

ROSS HOUSE, GRIMSBY DN31 3SW.

Our Ref: CW0064

14 April

Mr T Ravenscroft
The Elms
Wenter Road
New Mills
High Peak
Derbyshire

Dear Mr Ravenscroft,

I write further to your letter dated the 10th April, regarding your complaint of a recent purchase of our Linda McCartney Deep Country Pies.

I would like to thank you for taking the time and trouble to write back to us regarding this matter and I am pleased that we have been able to restore your confidence in our vegetarian products.

For your information a vegetarian dog food called Best, produced by Oscar Pet Foods has been launched. Should you wish to contact them, their address is:-

Oscar Pet Foods
Bannister Hall Mill
Higher Walton
Preston
Lancs
PR54DB

Please find enclosed with our compliments the enclosed vouchers to the value of £5.00 as a gesture of our concern and goodwill to enable you to purchase products of your choice from our extensive range.

Yours sincerely

Mrs Angie Wilding
Customer Care

Your ref CW0064

The Elms
Wenter Road
New Mills
High Peak
Derbyshire

Angie Wilding
McVitie's Prepared Foods
Ross House
Grimsby
DN31 3SW

24th April

Dear Angie Wilding

I just thought I'd let you know that I took your advice and purchased some Best vegetarian dog food and tried it out on our dog Rantzen. I'm happy to report that the following day he bit the postman, so it would seem that it is keeping him just as sharp as his usual Chum. Actually, I tried a couple of spoonfuls of it myself and found it to be quite indistinguishable from Linda McCartney Sausages. Whether or not I will be able to put up with Rantzen eating vegetarian dog food is another matter, as it appears to have made him quite flatulent. I had a word about it with Oscar Pet Foods and they said that this was normal and that he would soon 'settle down'. I hope so, while we still have some paint on the walls.

Actually, since upping my intake of Linda McCartney products I've had a few problems in that area myself. Apart from trying to look innocent and pretending it's somebody else, is there anything that can be done about this? Or, like Rantzen, will I soon settle down?

Yours sincerely

T Ravenscroft (Mr)

ROSS HOUSE, GRIMSBY DN31 3SW.

Our Ref: AW/CS

30 April

Mr T Ravenscroft
The Elms
Wenter Road
New Mills
High Peak
Derbyshire

Dear Mr Ravenscroft,

Thank you for your recent letter, I was very pleased to hear that you managed to find the Vegetarian Dog Food which we informed you about.

It is known that people that are not used to soya and vegetable proteins in their diet sometimes suffer with flatulence or similar symptoms at first, but once the body gets used to the foods in the system, this will settle down.

I would like to thank you once again for taking the time and trouble to write to us and I hope that you will continue to enjoy our range of Linda McCartney Foods.

Yours sincerely

Mrs Angie Wilding
Customer Care

The Elms
Wenter Road
New Mills
High Peak
Derbyshire

The Jacob's Bakery Ltd
P.O. Box 1   4th April
Long Lane
Liverpool
L9 7BQ

Dear Jacob's Bakery

I am writing to you in my official capacity as secretary of the New Mills Invalids Club. This year marks the 25th anniversary of the club, and we mean to celebrate the occasion in some style, whilst at the same time giving club funds a much-needed boost. To achieve this, we intend to manufacture and sell to the general public a chocolate biscuit. We are confident that we have the expertise to accomplish this as four of our members used to work for the local sweet and confectionery factory – in fact, it was because they worked at the local sweet and confectionery factory that they became invalids, having caught various parts of their anatomy in the machinery, but that's another matter.

Here is where you come in. I have long been a fan of your Jacob's Club biscuits, as have many of my fellow members, and to this end we would like to 'cash in' on your esteemed name by calling our biscuit a 'Jacob's Club Foot' biscuit. This would at once inform the public that it is a quality product, and also that it supports invalids. Can I have your permission, please?

Yours faithfully

T Ravenscroft (Mr)

17 April

Mr T Ravenscroft
The Elms
Wenter Road
New Mills
High Peak
Derbyshire

Dear Sir,

Thank you for your letter of 4th April requesting consent to bring out
a chocolate-covered biscuit called "Club Foot" in connection with
your society's forthcoming anniversary.

We have no objections to the proposals in your letter and hope it
proves to be a successful fund-raiser.

Our agreement is given on the understanding that you restrict sales
to local fund-raising events for a limited period and no mention of
The Jacob's Bakery Limited is made on the packaging etc.

Yours sincerely,
For and on behalf of The Jacob's Bakery Limited.

Gary Brookes
Legal & Finance Dept.

The Jacob's Bakery Limited
P.O. Box 1, Long Lane, Liverpool L9 7BQ

Registered in England No. 2322741. Registered Office: Long Lane, Aintree, Liverpool, L9 7LD

A **DANONE** GROUP COMPANY

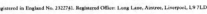

The Elms
Wenter Road
New Mills
High Peak
Derbyshire

Gary Brookes
Legal & Finance Dept   28th April
The Jacob's Bakery Ltd
P.O. Box 1
Long Lane
Liverpool
L9 7BQ

Dear Gary Brookes

Thank you for your letter of 17th April.

The New Mills Invalids Club will be forever in your debt. I take note of your request that we do not mention The Jacob's Bakery Limited on our packaging. In fact, I have gone one better, and have made absolutely sure that no one will be under any illusions that our biscuits have anything to do with The Jacob's Bakery, as you will see from a perusal of a facsimile of our wrapper, enclosed. It was designed by our Mr Hargreaves, who has one arm and an NVQ in graphic design, and I am sure you will agree he has made an excellent job of it.

Yours sincerely

T Ravenscroft (Mr)

Definitely nothing to do with the Jacob's Bakery Limited

JACOB'S

CLUB
FOOT

9 May

Mr T Ravenscroft
The Elms
Wenter Road
New Mills
High Peak
Derbyshire

Dear Sir,

Thank you for your letter of 28th April. As mentioned previously in my letter of 17th April, I would prefer it if no mention was made of The Jacob's Bakery Limited on the packaging.

Therefore, please could you remove from the packaging the statement "definitely nothing to do with The Jacob's Bakery Limited".

Yours sincerely,

Gary Brookes
Legal & Finance Dept.

The Jacob's Bakery Limited
P.O. Box 1, Long Lane, Liverpool L9 7BQ
Registered in England No. 2322741. Registered Office: Long Lane, Aintree, Liverpool, L9 7LD

A **DANONE** GROUP COMPANY

The Elms
Wenter Road
New Mills
High Peak
Derbyshire

Gary Brookes
Legal & Finance Dept   12th May
The Jacob's Bakery Ltd
P.O. Box 1
Long Lane
Liverpool
L9 7BQ

Dear Gary Brookes

Thank you for your letter of 9th May. Unfortunately, it arrived too late for me to alter the wording on our 'Club Foot' wrapper, so we went ahead with it as it was.

Our anniversary was last Saturday and I am happy to report that it was an unqualified success, especially chocolate biscuit-wise. We made a total of 5,000 biscuits and each and every one was sold. Not only that, the biscuits were enjoyed by all who bought them; in fact one man went so far as to say that our Club Foot biscuit was better than your Club biscuit, but I think he was just being nice to us, and anyway he isn't long out of the mental hospital and there are some who hold that he should never have been discharged.

I can report that the occasion was such a great success that we hope to make it an annual event. In closing, I and my fellow members would like to thank you from the bottom of our hearts (except for Mr Beasley, who has recently had a heart transplant, so he would like to thank you from the bottom of somebody else's heart).

Yours sincerely

T Ravenscroft (Mr)

9 June

Mr T Ravenscroft
The Elms
Wenter Road
New Mills
High Peak
Derbyshire

Dear Mr Ravenscroft,

Thank you for your letter of 12th May. I am glad that your product proved to be such a great success and I hope it raised a substantial amount of money for your society.

It is a shame that we did not receive a sample of your product to show to our R&D department! May I take this opportunity to wish you every success with your future fund-raising events.

Yours sincerely,

Gary Brookes
Legal & Finance Dept.

The Jacob's Bakery Limited
P.O. Box 1, Long Lane, Liverpool L9 7BQ

Registered in England No. 2322741. Registered Office: Long Lane, Aintree, Liverpool, L9 7LD

A DANONE GROUP COMPANY

The Elms
Wenter Road
New Mills
High Peak
Derbyshire

John West Foods Ltd
Liverpool   14th April
L3 9SR

Dear John West

I am suffering from a personal medical condition of which I
will spare you the details. However, my doctor says it might
help if I cut down on my salt intake. Unfortunately, I just love
anchovies, and especially John West Anchovies in Olive Oil,
which are, of course, extremely salty. I really wouldn't like to
forego my daily tin of anchovies if it can be avoided, and with
this in mind, I was wondering if you do a low-salt or salt-free
version?

Yours faithfully

T Ravenscroft (Mr)

JOHN WEST

JOHN WEST FOODS LIMITED
West House, Bixteth Street, Liverpool, L3 9SR.
Telephone
Telex

KW/DLF

21st April

Mr T Ravenscroft
The Elms
Wenter Road
New Mills
High Peak
Derbyshire

Dear Mr Ravenscroft

Thank you for your letter of 14th April and apologies
for the delay in reply due to business travel.

I regret that we do not do a low salt or salt free
anchovy. It is important to have the right salt levels
to preserve the product and a free salt version would
have to be a fully retorted product becoming a product
like Brisling or Sardines.

I am sorry therefore we cannot help at this time.

Yours sincerely

KEITH WILSON
MARKET MANAGER

The Elms
Wenter Road
New Mills
High Peak
Derbyshire

Keith Wilson
John West Foods Ltd   24th April
West House
Bixteth Street
Liverpool
L3 9SR

Dear Keith Wilson

Thank you for your letter of 21st April.

It seems that in order to enlist your help I will have to come clean about my personal medical condition. Your being a man is a big help, God knows what I would have done had you been a woman. The thing is I am having trouble 'performing', if you know what I mean. Now I like sex as much as I like anchovies, so you can imagine my dilemma. With this in mind, perhaps you can see your way to helping me?

It looks like I will have to obtain some 'fully retorted' anchovies, whatever that means. If I could get hold of some anchovies, would I be able to fully retort them myself?

I look forward to hearing from you.

Yours sincerely

T Ravenscroft (Mr)

JOHN WEST

IOHN WEST FOODS LIMITED
West House, Bixteth Street, Liverpool, L3 9SR.
Telephone
Telex

KW/DLF

29th April

Mr T Ravenscroft
The Elms
Wenter Road
New Mills
High Peak
Derbyshire

Dear Mr Ravenscroft

Thank you for your further letter of 24th April. I am sorry to learn of your problem but do not feel we can be of any further assistance.

The raw material is caught and processed in Spain, Portugal, Italy, Morocco and South America and therefore we do not receive raw material here in the UK.

I can only suggest you soak the current pack of Anchovies in milk to lessen the salt content which may make the product acceptable to your dilemma.

Yours sincerely

KEITH WILSON
MARKET MANAGER

The Elms
Wenter Road
New Mills
High Peak
Derbyshire

Keith Wilson
John West Foods Ltd   12th May
West House
Bixteth Street
Liverpool
L3 9SR

Dear Keith Wilson

Thank you for your letter of 29th April.

I am trying your idea of soaking your anchovies in milk, but thus far it has only been a partial success, inasmuch as that although it satisfies my craving for anchovies, I am still unable to fulfil my marital obligations. Up to now.

I have something quite odd to report, however. Rather than waste the milk in which the anchovies have soaked, I have been putting it down for the cat, and what only a few weeks ago was a shagged-out old tom now has a definite glint in his eye and has taken to stopping out all night once more. He has never had anchovy-flavoured milk before of course, and there is no doubt in my mind that it is this which has perked him up. I'll let you know if there are any developments as you might be on to a winner here.

In the meantime, it has occurred to me that where John West's Anchovies in Olive Oil are concerned, there are no economies to be made. What I mean is that when I buy beans, I buy them in big cans, which are more economical than small cans. So given my passion for anchovies, I would prefer to buy bigger cans of them, thus saving myself some money. Why isn't this possible?

Yours sincerely

T Ravenscroft (Mr)

JOHN WEST FOODS LIMITED
West House, Bixteth Street, Liverpool, L3 9SR.
Telephone
Telex

KW/DLF

14th May

Mr T Ravenscroft
The Elms
Wenter Road
New Mills
High Peak
Derbyshire

Dear Mr Ravenscroft

The final bit of help I can give you is to advise that
we have just launched a 100g Anchovies in Glass Jar.

These will shortly be available in Tesco and Sainsburys
and hopefully other stores as we continue to launch this
product.

Yours sincerely

KEITH WILSON
MARKET MANAGER

The Elms
Wenter Road
New Mills
High Peak
Derbyshire

Keith Wilson
John West Foods Ltd   19th May
West House
Bixteth Street
Liverpool
L3 9SR

Dear Keith Wilson

I am sorry to hear that you are leaving John West, and thank
you for the final bit of advice you were able to give me. Good
luck with your new job. I enclose a small donation of five
pounds towards your leaving present.

Unfortunately, I have refused to shop at Sainsburys for a while
now, and I'm not on very good terms with Tesco either, so I
won't be able to take advantage of your 100g Anchovies in
Glass Jar. Perhaps your successor could advise me of any other
outlets you are considering?

I am persisting with the milk-soaked anchovies and I am
definitely feeling a bit friskier. It looks like this could turn out
to be the best tip I have ever had, particularly as the cat is
going from strength to strength on anchovy-flavoured milk,
and has got the corner shop's tabby pregnant, according to the
owner.

Thank you for all your help.

Yours sincerely

T Ravenscroft (Mr)

 **JOHN WEST FOODS LIMITED**
West House, Bixteth Street, Liverpool, L3 9SR
Telephone
Telex

Our Ref: KW/Raven/DM

22 May

Mr T Ravenscroft
The Elms
Wenter Road
New Mills
High Peak
Derbyshire

Dear Mr Ravenscroft

Thank you for your cheque for £5 but there is a misunderstanding as I am not leaving John West.

I therefore return your kind donation and wish you well for the future.

Yours sincerely

Keith Wilson

The Elms
Wenter Road
New Mills
High Peak
Derbyshire

27th May

Keith Wilson
John West Foods Ltd
West House
Bixteth Street
Liverpool
L3 9SR

Dear Keith Wilson

Sorry about the misunderstanding, but because you said in your letter of 14th May that it was the final bit of help you could give me, I naturally assumed you were leaving John West's, as I found it difficult to believe that someone who had previously been so helpful would suddenly refuse to give help, especially to a good customer.

Anyway, I'm glad we've got it sorted out because you now may be able to help me in a big way, as your idea of soaking anchovies in milk is proving to be the best idea since sliced bread. I have only been on them for four weeks and already I can fulfil my marital obligations, and then some! In fact, my wife says it's like being on honeymoon again. (I hope not because I got her pregnant!) When you also take into account what has happened to our cat, who continues to terrorise the neighbourhood's feline population, there can be no doubt that milk-soaked anchovies possess outstanding aphrodisiac qualities. This is bound to be of tremendous interest to lovers of anchovies and lovers of sex alike, and even those who don't like the former could very well be prepared to put up with them if they gave them a sporting chance of getting more of the latter.

Bearing in mind the above, I am considering marketing Milk-Soaked Anchovies as a sex aid, and I would be grateful to you if you could let me know your best price for anchovies in 100-kg barrels, or whatever they come in; or failing that, the name of your suppliers abroad so that I may do business with them direct.

Yours sincerely

T Ravenscroft (Mr)

The Elms
Wenter Road
New Mills
High Peak
Derbyshire

CWS Ltd
MANCHESTER   20th March
M60 4ES

Dear CWS

The Co-op haven't often given me cause to praise their products, your foodstuffs being more synonymous with convenience rather than Epicurean delights, but I must say that with your Egg Lasagne you are right up there with Marks and Spencers. Coming from me this is praise indeed, as I have something of a reputation as a lasagne buff. However, and with hand on my heart, I can honestly say that your lasagne was the second most enjoyable I have ever tasted, bested only by the truly mouth-watering lasagne served to the fortunate passengers of Air 2000, which is well worth the price of the flight alone. (I once tried to obtain the recipe from them, but they wouldn't give it to me, so no fools them!)

Have you any other products in the same range? Even if they are only half as good as your lasagne, I would be very keen to try them.

Yours faithfully

T Ravenscroft (Mr)

P.O. Box 53
New Century House
Manchester M60 4ES

Our Ref: 195215

25 March

Mr T Ravenscroft
The Elms
Wenter Road
New Mills
High Peak
Derbyshire

Dear Mr Ravenscroft,

Thank you for letting me know about your recent purchase of Co-op Egg Lasagne.

We make every effort to ensure our products meet the high standards that we specify and I am very sorry that on this occasion you have been disappointed.

We do routinely check all our suppliers to ensure that the high standards we insist upon are being met and we shall be informing them of your complaint.

As a token of my regret I have enclosed gift vouchers to the value of £2.00 for any inconvenience incurred, and I hope that this unfortunate incident has not prevented you from shopping at your local Co-op. If I can be of any further assistance, please do not hesitate to contact me.

Yours sincerely

Jean Jackson
Customer Relations

The Elms
Wenter Road
New Mills
High Peak
Derbyshire

Your ref 195215

1st April

Jean Jackson
CWS Ltd
PO Box 53
New Century House
MANCHESTER
M60 4ES

Dear Jean Jackson

Thank you for your letter of 25th March. Your reply really does beggar belief! I wrote to you in praise of one of your products and you replied with a letter of apology! This worries me more than somewhat, as it would indicate that you at the Co-op receive so many letters of complaint that regardless of its contents you rattle off an apology in reply to every letter you receive. Please reassure me that this isn't the case, before my confidence in your company is destroyed forever. And you still haven't answered my original query, so I will repeat it. Have you any other products in the same range as your Egg Lasagne?

Yours sincerely

T Ravenscroft (Mr)

P.O. Box 53
New Century House
Manchester M60 4ES

Our Ref: 195215

3 April

Mr T Ravenscroft
The Elms
Wenter Road
New Mills
High Peak
Derbyshire

Dear Mr Ravenscroft,

Thank you for your letter regarding Co-op Egg Lasagne. Firstly may I apologise for the error in my original reply to you.

We are happy that you are pleased with this product and you may be sure that we will do everything possible to maintain the quality and value in accordance with your kind remarks.

The other products available in this range are as follows:-

Co-op Lasagne Verdi, Co-op Lasagne and Co-op Tagliatelle.

If you have any other comments, or I can be of any help in the future, please do not hesitate to contact me.

Yours sincerely

Jean Jackson
Customer Relations

The Elms
Wenter Road
New Mills
High Peak
Derbyshire

Your ref 195215

7th April

Jean Jackson
CWS Ltd
PO Box 53
New Century House
Manchester
M60 4ES

Dear Jean Jackson

Thank you for your letter. Since I last wrote to you, something quite exciting has happened! As I mentioned to you in my original letter, I am something of a lasagne nut, and when you have read the following words, you will realise the reason for my excitement, as it seems I may have made something of a breakthrough in the field of lasagne technology.

Last Friday, I had to make one of my frequent flights to the Czech Republic on business. Now I don't know if you are at all familiar with the food served upon CSK Czechoslovak Airlines, but it is not to be recommended. (Incidentally, on no account let any of the cabin staff get anywhere near your false teeth.) To avoid the airline's food, I usually take a sandwich, but on this occasion the bread bin was empty, so I had to think of something else. Now I don't know why, other than the fact that I am lasagne mad, but I then had the brainwave of heating up one of your Co-op Egg Lasagnes and putting it in a thermos flask. It was a bit tricky spooning it in, and it did cause quite a few stares from my fellow passengers when I upended the flask and shook out the lasagne on to a plate, but the time and effort were well worth it. Whether it had something to do with the cabin pressure, or whether it was because it had spent some time in a thermos flask, I don't know; but what I do know without any shadow of doubt is that your lasagne from a flask at 30,000 feet is in a different class, indeed the equal to the lasagne of Air 2000! Believe me, it was like eating ambrosia. (The food of the Gods, that is, not the rice pudding, which can be quite nice, but in my experience somewhat inconsistent.)

Following the experience, I tried out an experiment at home. First I heated up another of your lasagnes and spooned it into a thermos flask, left it for a few hours, then tried it. It was the equal of the lasagne I had had on the aeroplane! I then enlisted the aid of a few neighbours and blind-tested your lasagne heated up in the normal manner, against your lasagne heated up then put into a thermos flask for several hours. Every one of the testers vastly preferred 'Egg Lasagne Thermos Flask'!

Bearing the above in mind, I think that you should seriously consider recommending this method of preparing your lasagne on the packet. Or maybe you could alter your manufacturing process to include your lasagne resting in a giant thermos flask for a few hours before packaging? What do you think?

Yours sincerely

T Ravenscroft (Mr)

CWS

P.O. Box 53
New Century House
Manchester M60 4ES

Our Ref: 195215

11 April

Mr T Ravenscroft
The Elms
Wenter Road
New Mills
High Peak
Derbyshire

Dear Mr Ravenscroft,

Thank you for your letter regarding Co-op Egg Lasagne.

I have noted your comments but do not know if this idea would be practical, however I will pass on your suggestion to the appropriate department for interest or action as necessary.

We were pleased to hear that you enjoy this product and enclosed with our compliments is a Goodwill Voucher for £2.00 to enable you to try other Co-op products.

Yours sincerely

Jean Jackson
Customer Relations

The Elms
Wenter Road
New Mills
High Peak
Derbyshire

Your ref 195215

16th April

Jean Jackson
CWS Ltd
PO Box 53
New Century House
MANCHESTER
M60 4ES

Dear Jean Jackson

I am not at all happy that you do not feel able to bring about an undoubted improvement in your Co-op Egg Lasagne. I am not at all happy about the reckless abandon with which you appear to throw about Goodwill Vouchers for £2.00 either. No wonder the Co-op can't afford to pay out divi any more!

Yours sincerely

T Ravenscroft (Mr)

The Elms
Wenter Road
New Mills
High Peak
Derbyshire

Butcher's Ltd
Baker Group House   22nd March
Crick
Northants
NN6 7TZ

Dear Sir

I am writing to congratulate you on a truly excellent product. I have just dined on a can of your Butcher's Tripe Mix, which I had with a portion of oven chips, and it was quite superb. With a bottle of Beaujolais to wash it down, it felt almost like I was back in the Dordogne. At long last a British manufacturer has succeeded in doing with offal what the French have been doing with it for years. God bless you!

I do, however, have one minor criticism. Why do you refer on the label to your tripe as an 'animal derivative'? Tripe is offal, nothing more, nothing less, and to call it anything else is to pretend that it is something it isn't. There is nothing wrong with offal, believe me, I've eaten tons of it, and I shall be eating even more tons of it if you keep up the standard of your wonderful Butcher's Tripe Mix. A question, though. Why is there a picture of a dog on the label?

Yours faithfully

T Ravenscroft (Mr)

BUTCHER'S
PET CARE

Butcher's Pet Care Ltd.
Baker Group House,
Crick,
Northants, NN6 7TZ

Our Ref:
Your Ref:

24th April

Mr T Ravenscroft
The Elms
Wenter Road
New Mills
High Peak
Derbyshire

Dear Mr Ravenscroft

Thank you for your letter congratulating us on our Butcher's Tripe Mix product.

We receive many similar letters from satisfied owners writing to us on behalf of their dog. Yours is the first letter we have had from a human consumer.

The Feeding Stuffs Regulations 1995 require us by law to describe tripe on the label under the heading meat and animal derivatives. The term offal is not permitted although as you point out it is nothing to be ashamed of.

Please remember Butcher's Tripe Mix is a complementary food and to keep your nose wet and coat in tip-top condition you must eat it mixed with an equal quantity of reputable mixer meal.

Please find enclosed £5 worth of vouchers towards your future purchases.

Yours sincerely

Ian Cresswell
Technical Manager

The Elms
Wenter Road
New Mills
High Peak
Derbyshire

Ian Cresswell
Butcher's Ltd
Baker Group House
Crick
Northants
NN6 7TZ

28th April

Dear Ian Cresswell

Thank you for your letter of 24th April, and the vouchers, which I passed on to the needy.

It would appear that I have made a mistake and that Butcher's Tripe Mix is a dog food! Perhaps it is an understandable mistake though; I mean on boxes of Kellogg's Frosties there's a picture of a tiger, but it would be a fool who claimed that tigers eat cornflakes, as I'm sure you would be the first to agree.

Getting back to the point, your letter arrived too late to have any influence on a meal I recently put on chez Ravenscroft for a potential client. However, I doubt it would have made any difference to the menu I had decided on, even if it had arrived before my client. In the event, he said that the Tripes Provençal, made with your Butcher's Tripe Mix as the basis, was quite superb, and he couldn't believe that most of it had come out of a can. In fact, when I showed him the can to prove it, he was quite speechless. If I don't get a big order out of him, I will be very surprised, although up to now he has been out of the office every time I've tried to contact him.

I must say I enjoyed your little joke about keeping my nose wet and my coat in tip-top condition. Very funny!

Yours sincerely

T Ravenscroft (Mr)

END OF CORRESPONDENCE

The Elms
Wenter Road
New Mills
High Peak
Derbyshire

Tesco Stores Ltd
Cheshunt
EN8 9SL

24th March

Dear Tesco

I have just finished a carton of your Healthy Eating Crème Fraiche D'Isigny, and very nice it was too. In fact, it was almost up to the standard of your regular Crème Fraiche D'Isigny, which I normally buy. Which brings me to the question: if your Healthy Eating Crème Fraiche D'Isigny is 'healthy eating' then, by definition, is your regular Crème Fraiche D'Isigny 'unhealthy eating'?

This is of no small concern to me because all things being equal I prefer your regular Crème Fraiche D'Isigny – try dipping oven chips in it, gorgeous – but not at the expense of my health.

Looking forward to hearing from you.

Yours faithfully

T Ravenscroft (Mr)

TESCO

Customer Service
PO Box 73
Baird Avenue
Dundee
DD1 9NF

3 April

Mr T Ravenscroft
The Elms
Wenter Road
New Mills
High Peak
Derbyshire

Dear Mr Ravenscroft

Thank you for your letter dated 24 March.

We are currently investigating this matter and will be contacting you again in the near future.

Thank you for taking the time to contact us.

Yours sincerely
For and on behalf of Tesco Stores Ltd

Martin Cunningham
Customer Services

The Elms
Wenter Road
New Mills
High Peak
Derbyshire

Martin Cunningham
Tesco   23rd April
PO Box 73
Baird Avenue
Dundee
DD1 9NF

Dear Martin Cunningham

It is now over three weeks since you wrote to me. How are your investigations coming along? I must say that you are dragging your heels somewhat on this one, the Co-op were much quicker off the mark when I wrote to them about their lasagne. *And* they sent me a voucher.

Yours sincerely

T Ravenscroft (Mr)

TESCO

Customer Service
PO Box 73
Baird Avenue
Dundee
DD1 9NF

29 April

Mr T Ravenscroft
The Elms
Wenter Road
New Mills
High Peak
Derbyshire

Dear Mr Ravenscroft

Thank you for your letter dated 24 March regarding Healthy Eating Crème Fraiche and please let me apologise for the delay in responding.

With regards your query, I contacted our technologist who explained that the Healthy Eating range is designed around a number of things: for example, most are half the fat, lower in sodium salt or lower in sugar than the normal products. Thus they are aimed at customers who want to reduce their intake of certain substances. This is not to say that the normal products are 'unhealthy', just that Healthy Eating products are a healthier option.

I hope this goes some way to answering your question and allays your fears about our non-Healthy Eating products. I hope you continue to enjoy our Crème Fraiche (with oven chips – may have to try that one!). Should you have any further queries do not hesitate to contact me.

Thank you for taking the time and trouble to write to us.

Yours sincerely
For and on behalf of Tesco Stores Ltd

Gary Brown
Customer Services Manager

The Elms
Wenter Road
New Mills
High Peak
Derbyshire

Gary Brown
Tesco   1st May
PO Box 73
Baird Avenue
Dundee
DD1 9NF

Dear Gary Brown

Thank you for your letter of 29th April.

I would suggest to you that your technologist is wasting his time at Tesco, for a successful career in politics as a spin doctor surely awaits him. If you are taking out quantities of fat, salt and sugar in order to make a product healthy, then it follows that fat, salt and sugar are bad for our health; therefore his sentence 'This is not to say that the normal products are unhealthy, just that Healthy Eating products are a healthier option' is not only double-speak, but one of the finest examples of double-speak I have seen for ages, and worthy of Tony Blair himself.

In truth, it would make more sense to call your two varieties of crème fraiche 'Unhealthy Eating' and 'Very Unhealthy Eating', but when was the last time a supermarket chain let the truth get in the way of a sale?

Yours sincerely

T Ravenscroft (Mr)

TESCO

Customer Service
PO Box 73
Baird Avenue
Dundee
DD1 9NF

7 May

Mr T Ravenscroft
The Elms
Wenter Road
New Mills
High Peak
Derbyshire

Dear Mr Ravenscroft

Thank you for your letter dated 1 May.

As far as our technologist is concerned I'm sure he does in fact write Tony Blair's speeches!! I think that the wording 'Healthy Eating' is a little misleading as all food is healthy as it provides essential fuel for our bodies, to keep us going throughout the day. We all need certain amounts of fat, sugar, salt etc. to keep us fit and healthy. Obviously different foods contain differing amounts of each. So, this dispels the theory that non-healthy eating products are by definition unhealthy.

The healthy eating label helps to provide people with a choice and serves to make their shopping trips easier. For example, people who suffer from high cholesterol, heart disease, or diabetes, may wish to reduce their intake of fat, sugar or salt. By highlighting our products which have reduced levels of these this makes their shopping and perhaps their lives easier.

Conversely, what may be a healthy diet for a person suffering one of the above mentioned problems may not be suitable for someone else. This has been highlighted in the news recently, where some parents have been feeding their children low fat diets which are unsuitable for a child's health and growth. Hence it has resulted in children who are malnourished or who have stunted growth. So, in this case the so-called normal products would have been the healthy option.

With regard to your closing comment, we are not totally sale oriented and, as has been illustrated, in being more customer focused by endeavouring to meet our customers needs, we are not lying to make a quick sale!

I hope this clears this up a little better. Thank you for taking the time and trouble to write to us.

Yours sincerely
For and on behalf of Tesco Stores Ltd

Gary Brown
Customer Services Manager

The Elms
Wenter Road
New Mills
High Peak
Derbyshire

Gary Brown
Tesco   12th May
PO Box 73
Baird Avenue
Dundee
DD1 9NF

Dear Gary Brown

Well, you've certainly put me in my place, and no mistake!
Not to say enlightened me. Particularly so with regard to
children's low-fat diets that are unsuitable for children's
growth. This probably explains why my wife and myself, each
brought up on roast and three veg, are both six-footers, whilst
our three children are of below average height. In fact, our
eldest, fifteen-year-old Marcus, is only four foot three. I can
see now that I shall have to get them all off Heinz Weight
Watcher Soups and Ambrosia Low-Fat Rice Pudding and get
them on to Big Macs and Syrup Pudding before I do any
permanent damage to them! Thank you for your valuable
advice. When I return from holiday next week, I shall be
writing a strong letter to Heinz and Ambrosia telling them that
you have informed me that their Weight Watcher Soup and
Low-Fat Rice Pudding products are unhealthy for children, and
that they would do well to point this out on their labels. But,
as an obviously concerned company, shouldn't you be
pointing this out too?

Yours sincerely

T Ravenscroft (Mr)

TESCO

Customer Service
PO Box 73
Baird Avenue
Dundee
DD1 9NF

15 May

Mr T Ravenscroft
The Elms
Wenter Road
New Mills
High Peak
Derbyshire

Dear Mr Ravenscroft

Thank you for your letter dated 12th of May.

Did you hear the Queen's speech yesterday? – Our technologist at his best, don't you think!

I was glad to read that you are a healthy six footer brought up on healthy meat and three. I have to say that I was also, but unfortunately only managed to reach an average five foot eight – more to do with my genes I think. I am sure if you write to Heinz or Ambrosia they will tell you exactly the same as I have with regards choice and providing for customers perhaps less fortunate, or healthy, than yourself.

I do not however think that feeding your children on Big Macs and Syrup Puddings will make them more healthy somehow, just as feeding them on Weight Watchers soup will not. You need to strike a balance between the two to provide a healthy diet for the individual concerned. Retailers and manufacturers alike provide the information to help customers to make the right choices, after that it is up to you.

To this end I have enclosed copies of the leaflets that Tesco's publish, and are available in stores, to help customers to make educated decisions about their diet.

I hope you have a good holiday and don't forget to send a postcard. Thank you for taking the time and trouble to write.

Yours sincerely
For and on behalf of Tesco Stores Ltd

Gary Brown
Customer Services Manager

Enc. All Healthy Eating Leaflets

The Elms
Wenter Road
New Mills
High Peak
Derbyshire

Gary Brown
Tesco
PO Box 73
Baird Avenue
Dundee
DD1 9NF

19th May

Dear Gary Brown

Thank you for the leaflets. However, I am not a child, nor am I elderly, and I am most certainly not pregnant – although my wife might soon be if milk-soaked anchovies continue to improve my sex drive at the rate they have been doing.

I will read the other leaflets with interest, especially your Healthy Eating Guide to Fat and Cholesterol, where I hope to find a Healthy Eating Meat and Potato Pie.

When on holiday I won't forget to send you a postcard, which will be rich in fibre.

Yours sincerely

T Ravenscroft (Mr)

END OF CORRESPONDENCE

The Elms
Wenter Road
New Mills
High Peak
Derbyshire

McCain Foods (GB) Ltd
Scarborough
North Yorkshire
YO11 3BS

27th March

Dear McCain Foods

I feel that the time is long overdue when I should write to you in praise of your McCain's Oven Chips. I honestly don't know what I would do without them. Well, I do, but as it involves the mind-numbing task of peeling potatoes, I would rather not think about it. The fact is that your oven chips are quite the best chips it has ever been my pleasure to eat, and as a Northerner I know my chips.

However, I can't say that I think much of your cooking instructions, so rather than cook them in the oven or under the grill as you suggest, which tends to make them rather dry, I cook them in the good old-fashioned way in a chip pan. This has the effect of making them much more succulent, believe me, especially when using good beef dripping as the frying medium.

The only thing that worries me about doing this is that there may be a possibility that the chip pan method of cooking oven chips uses more fat. Have my worries any foundation in fact or am I being overcautious?

Yours faithfully

T Ravenscroft (Mr)

AC/SY

4 April

Mr T Ravenscroft
The Elms
Wenter Road
New Mills
High Peak
Derbyshire

Dear Mr Ravenscroft

Thank you for your letter letting us know how you cook McCain Oven Chips.

As our Oven Chips are fried in Sunflower Oil, and then you are frying them in dripping, you are nearly doubling the amount of fat on the chips.

If you wish to fry our chips, me we recommend that you try some of our fry chips and we have enclosed a £1.00 McCain voucher to enable you to do so.

Yours sincerely

Ann Charlton (Mrs)

CONSUMER SERVICES MANAGER

Enc

The Elms
Wenter Road
New Mills
High Peak
Derbyshire

Your ref AC/SY

10th April

Ann Charlton
Consumer Services Manager
McCain Foods (GB) Ltd
Havers Hill
Scarborough
North Yorkshire
YO11 3BS

Dear Ann Charlton

Thank you for your letter of 4th April and the voucher.

I tried some of your fry chips, but quite frankly found them to be a bit of a disappointment when compared with your oven chips. If I were you, I would discontinue them and just sell oven chips, with something like 'Even Better Fried In Beef Dripping!' emblazoned on the packaging.

Incidentally, and with reference to the final sentence of your letter, when wishing to indicate that both yourself and your compatriots recommend something, it is only necessary to say 'we' and not 'me we', as you appear to think. Or is this an example of the Yorkshire dialect?

Yours sincerely

T Ravenscroft (Mr)

The Elms
Wenter Road
New Mills
High Peak
Derbyshire

The Ryvita Company Ltd
Old Wareham Road   1st April
Poole
Dorset
BH12 4QW

Dear Ryvita

Despite being in my forties, I have just tried Ryvita for the very
first time. What a revelation! Since first sampling the biscuits
not much more than a week ago I have already devoured six
packets! I eat them two at a time thickly spread with butter
with about a dozen oven chips in between as part of a calorie-
controlled diet. The only fault I find with them is that they
tend to make the roof of my mouth sore. Would your Oat Bran
or Dark Rye versions be any more forgiving?

Yours faithfully

T Ravenscroft (Mr)

Mr T Ravenscroft
The Elms
Wenter Road
New Mills
High Peak
Derbyshire

The Ryvita Company Limited
Old Wareham Road, Poole, Dorset BH12 4QW

24 April

Dear Mr Ravenscroft

Thank you for your letter of 1st April and please accept my sincere apologies for the delay in responding.

We are absolutely delighted that you have discovered Ryvita and are intrigued at a calorie controlled diet which includes regular helpings of Ryvita Chip Butties!

With reference to your particular queries, Ryvita is 100% natural and contains no artificial additives or preservatives. The ingredients are purely wholemeal rye, water and a pinch of salt. Ryvita is therefore naturally high in fibre and low in fat and contains a natural balance of vitamins and minerals. As such, Ryvita is the ideal product to be incorporated into any healthy eating plan and is widely recommended by nutritionists and slimming clubs. However, if you are generally concerned about your diet, we would recommend that you see your doctor who is the best person to advise you on the suitability of your diet.

As Ryvita is baked at fairly high temperatures, it is naturally very crunchy, but there are many toppings you can use to help soften the crispbread which are also delicious and very nutritious. We have enclosed some booklets on Ryvita toppings and serving suggestions to give you some ideas.

In addition, we also manufacture an extruded crispbread called "Crackerbread". Crackerbread has a "softer" bite than Ryvita and we are enclosing a pack for you to try. Crackerbread, like Ryvita, is available from all major multiples.

We do hope this gives you lots of ideas and good luck with the diet.

With kind regards

Yours sincerely

Cathy Dalton
Product Manager

The Ryvita No Diet Diet

Breakfasts

Daily Dash
1 cereal bowl of high fibre cereal with a good splash of semi-skimmed milk and 1 small sliced banana or 4 prunes. 3 slices of Dark Rye Ryvita with 1 tbsp of low fat soft cheese and a little reduced sugar blackcurrant jam.

Pack Up and Go
5 slices of Original Ryvita topped with thinly sliced reduced fat cheese such as Dutch Edam (40g/1½oz) and tomato slices (toasted if liked) and 2 satsumas or 2 plums.

Egg Head
4 slices of Multi-Grain Ryvita or 2 slices of wholemeal bread or toast with a scrape of low fat spread & 1 egg - boiled or scrambled in a non-stick pan. Serve with ½ a pink grapefruit.

Winter Warmer
1 bowl of porridge made with a mix of semi-skimmed milk and water, with a sprinkling of raisins. 1 slice of wholemeal toast or a couple of slices of Ryvita, with a little marmalade.

Bacon Medley
6 slices of Original Ryvita or 2 slices of wholemeal bread spread with tomato ketchup or brown sauce and topped with 2 rashers of well grilled lean bacon, grilled mushrooms and tomato slices.

Lunches

Crunchy Green Salad
Make up a mixed green salad with 1 tbsp of grated parmesan, 25g/1oz of diced ham and 1 tbsp of reduced calorie salad dressing. Serve with Ryvita croutons and a small bread roll or 4 Ryvita.
To make Ryvita Croutons - spread a Ryvita with low fat garlic and herb flavour cheese and crumble onto salad.

Tempting Tuna
6 slices of Ryvita or 2 slices of wholemeal bread piled high with tuna salad (made with ½ a regular can of tuna fish in brine (drained), mixed with 2 tsps low calorie mayonnaise, diced onion and red pepper). Top with cucumber slices.

Go Greek
Top 6 slices of Sesame Ryvita or 2 slices of wholemeal bread with 6 wafer thin slices of smoked ham, cucumber and tomato slices. Top with a drizzle of low fat natural yoghurt.

Melting Jacket
Pile a medium sized jacket potato with 2 heaped tbsps of low fat grated cheese and 2 heaped tbsps of low fat fromage frais. Add a sprinkling of chopped spring onions. Serve with a mixed salad.

The Elms
Wenter Road
New Mills
High Peak
Derbyshire

Cathy Dalton
The Ryvita Company Ltd
Old Wareham Road
Poole
Dorset
BH1 4QW

6th May

Dear Cathy Dalton

Thank you for your letter of 24th April and the packets of Crackerbread. Thank you also for the booklets, especially the No Diet Diet. At the time of writing, I have been on your Daily Dash breakfast for a week, and by now I certainly know why you've called it the Daily Dash. I'm going to try your Pack Up and Go next week and if its name turns out to be equally appropriate, I am certainly not going to forget where the lavatory is. I have also tried Tempting Tuna and can report that if you cut out the low-calorie mayonnaise and replace it with a generous portion of oven chips, it is even more tempting. You might like to include it when you compile your next booklet? You could call it Tempting Providence.

Yours sincerely

T Ravenscroft (Mr)

The Elms
Wenter Road
New Mills
High Peak
Derbyshire

H J Heinz Co Ltd
Hayes   2nd April
Middlesex
UB4 8AL

Dear H J Heinz

I am afraid I have a rather serious complaint to make about your Thomas The Tank Engine And Friends Pasta Shapes.

Yesterday, I opened a can of the said concoction for my youngest's lunch. On giving it to him, he immediately went a bright shade of red and started screaming. Then, and completely without warning, he hurled the entire contents of the bowl at the kitchen wall. I would respectfully point out that on the can it clearly states that the pasta shapes contained within include, amongst others, Thomas The Tank Engine, Harold The Helicopter, Trevor The Tractor and The Fat Controller. My complaint, and the reason for my two-year-old's eccentric behaviour, is that the can didn't contain so much as a single Fat Controller, which happens to be young Oscar's favourite. (He likes to bite his head off.)

You can take the can's lack of Fat Controllers as gospel as I had to remove every one of the sixty-five pasta pieces from the kitchen wall. For what it's worth, I counted twenty-two Thomas The Tank Engines, eleven Harold The Helicopters, seven Trevor The Tractors, ten Bertie The Buses, nine unspecified items which slightly resembled bridges or signal boxes, and six unspecified items which were unidentifiable, but certainly weren't the Fat Controller, at least not unless Thomas The Tank Engine had just run over him.

From the time I placed the bowl of Thomas The Tank Engine And Friends Pasta Shapes in front of young Oscar until the time I had restored the kitchen floor to its former pristine condition, including settling down Oscar and cleaning the kitchen wall, took up an hour of my very valuable time. This was completely due to your negligence and I would like to know what you intend to do about it.

Yours faithfully

T Ravenscroft (Mr)

H. J. Heinz Company Limited

Hayes Park
Hayes
Middlesex UB4 8AL.

0335827A

Mr T Ravenscroft   8 April
The Elms
Wenter Road
New Mills
High Peak
Derbyshire

Dear Mr Ravenscroft,

Thank you for letting us know of your experience with
our Thomas The Tank Spaghetti. We are concerned to
learn that one of our products did not meet our
normal high standards.

The greatest care is taken to ensure that our
products reach our customers in perfect condition
and tests are carried out by our staff at every stage
during preparation and manufacture. Our procedures
are approved and regularly audited by independent
authorities. It is apparent from your comments,
however, that a filling fault has occurred in this
instance.

As you would expect, we take our responsibilities to
our customers very seriously indeed. Thank you for
your help in supplying information about your
complaint: this is used to help us in our programme
of continuous improvement of our equipment and
quality procedures.

We are sorry you have had this experience with our
product. Please accept the enclosed in accordance
with our guarantee to refund the price of the product
if it does not meet your requirements. We hope your
confidence in our products has been restored and
that we will continue to receive your valued custom.

Yours sincerely,

Helen Reeves
Consumer Contact

Enc: £2.00 Voucher

Your ref 0335827A

Helen Reeves
H J Heinz Co Ltd
Hayes Park
Hayes
Middlesex
UB4 8AL

The Elms
Wenter Road
New Mills
High Peak
Derbyshire

10th April

Dear Helen Reeves

Thank you for your letter of 8th April.

It is nice to know that you take such care to ensure that your products reach your customers in perfect condition. Unfortunately, I am having great difficulty in believing you. The reason for this is your inexplicable reference to 'Thomas The Tank'. I would respectfully point out to you that Thomas is not a tank, but a tank engine, and it seems to me that if you at Heinz can't tell the difference between a tank and a tank engine, then there is little chance of you being able to tell the difference between Bertie The Bus and The Fat Controller, and if this is the case, you are going to have many more cans lacking Fat Controllers. I just hope I am not unfortunate enough to serve up one of them to young Oscar, or it will be kitchen wall cleaning time again! Which brings me to the voucher for £2 that you enclosed, which I am returning to you as I regard it as an insult. If this was meant to compensate me for the time I spent cleaning my kitchen, then it is totally inadequate. Good Lord, woman, it cost me almost that much in Flash alone.

For the record, a tank is a large military vehicle, which runs on tracks and has a big gun at the front. A tank engine is a wheeled traction vehicle used on the railway to pull carriages.

Yours sincerely

T Ravenscroft (Mr)

H. J. Heinz Company Limited

Hayes Park
Hayes
Middlesex UB4 8AL

Our Ref: 0335827A

Mr T Ravenscroft
The Elms
Wenter Road
New Mills
High Peak
Derbyshire

22nd April

Dear Mr Ravenscroft,

We were sorry to learn that you are unhappy with our original response to your complaint about a lack of "Fat Controllers" in a tin of Thomas the Tank Engine and Friends Pasta Shapes

We note that you were unhappy with our reimbursement. However it is our policy to ensure that all our consumers are refunded for any product which they feel does not meet their expectations. Our vouchers were intended to reflect this and we are sorry you chose not to accept them.

Yours sincerely

Brian Hooker
CONSUMER CONTACT MANAGER

Your ref 0335827A

Brian Hooker
H J Heinz Co Ltd
Hayes Park
Hayes
Middlesex
UB4 8AL

The Elms
Wenter Road
New Mills
High Peak
Derbyshire

23rd April

Dear Brian Hooker

The reason I found your original response inadequate was not because I was unhappy about your reimbursement – I am not a man who seeks nor needs charity – but because you at Heinz don't seem to know the difference between a tank and a tank engine. I really expected more from one of our leading food manufacturers.

I have now realised why you came up with the slogan 'Heinz 57 Varieties'. It is quite obviously some legal ploy – 'varieties' being a suitably vague enough expression to cater for the eccentricities of your can-filling machinery, and 57 of them to cover you in the event of your mistaking a tank engine for any of 56 other large locomotives.

Yours sincerely

T Ravenscroft (Mr)

The Elms
Wenter Road
New Mills
High Peak
Derbyshire

Interpet Ltd
Vincent Lane   8th April
Dorking
Surrey
RH4 3YK

Dear Interpet

As a fishpond owner, I am never without a supply of your product 3 Seasons Floating Food Hoops. The other day, my wife accidentally served a portion of them to my middle son Henry, in mistake for Kellogg's Honey Nut Loops, which are very similar in appearance. Far from complaining about it, Henry wolfed down the lot, and with even more gusto than usual, then enquired as to what the 'super new breakfast cereal' was and could he have it regularly.

I must say that I don't share my son's opinion of the taste of your Floating Food Hoops – I tried a spoonful, and to me they taste like rabbit hutches – but then what appeals to the palate of a child has never ceased to amaze me since the advent of the fish finger. However, the way I see it is that if he wants to eat fish food, that's his kettle of fish – or rather his bowl of 3 Seasons Floating Food Hoops – so good luck to him. However, before I give him my blessing, I thought it would be prudent to check with you to ensure that there isn't anything in your product that might be harmful to human children.

I look forward to hearing from you.

Yours faithfully

T Ravenscroft (Mr)

The Elms
Wenter Road
New Mills
High Peak
Derbyshire

Interpet Ltd
Vincent Lane   28th April
Dorking
Surrey
RH4 3YX

Dear Interpet

I would refer you to a letter that I sent to you on 8th April. I really expected an answer before now. Indeed, if my Japanese Koi fish had to wait as long for their 3 Seasons Floating Food Hoops as I have had to wait for an answer from you, they would have become 'floaters' long ago.

So please, my boy Henry is back on the Kellogg's Honey Nut Loops again and consequently is making my life a misery with his pestering.

Yours faithfully

T Ravenscroft (Mr)

INTERPET

Vincent Lane, Dorking, Surrey RH4 3

Mr T Ravenscroft
The Elms
Wenter Road
New Mills
High Peak
Derbyshire

6 May
JEP/cc

Dear Mr Ravenscroft

Thank you for your recent correspondence and we would offer our sincere apologies for the delay in responding to you. Unfortunately, our research scientist has been absent from the office and we needed to clarify the situation with him.

Although the product is harmless, we cannot advise or recommend it for human consumption. We would therefore suggest that Henry continues with Kellogg's Honey Nut Loops.

Once again, please accept our apologies for the delay.

Yours sincerely

Julie Parker
<u>Customer Services Administrator</u>

The Elms
Wenter Road
New Mills
High Peak
Derbyshire

Julie Parker
Interpet Lt   8th May
Vincent Lane
Dorking
Surrey
RH4 3YX

Dear Julie Parker

Thank you for your letter of 6th May.

Since writing to you, there has been a development. Apparently, Henry has been eating your Floating Food Hoops behind my back ever since I first wrote to you on 8th April! It appears that the young shaver has been taking a handful out of the container into which I dole the daily ration for feeding to my Koi, then mixing it in with his Honey Nut Loops. (I only found out when I became suspicious because the fish always seemed to be hungry.) When I showed him your letter, he begged me to disregard it, and pleaded with me to be allowed to continue eating Floating Food Hoops, pointing out that he hasn't suffered any ill effects, so why not? In fact, he has never looked fitter, and he swears that his swimming has improved, although whether that is due to eating fish food or just that he is a growing lad is debatable.

Bearing the above in mind, I am loathe to stop him eating Floating Food Hoops, and to this end, I would be interested to know why you can't recommend them for human consumption if, as you say, they are harmless?

Yours sincerely

T Ravenscroft (Mr)

INTERPET

Vincent Lane, Dorking, Surrey RH4 3Y

Mr T Ravenscroft
The Elms
Wenter Road
New Mills
High Peak
Derbyshire

20 May
JEP/cc

Dear Mr Ravenscroft

Thank you for your further letter dated 8 May regarding our Floating Food Hoops.

We are delighted that Henry enjoys the product so much! However, we can only reiterate what we stated in our previous letter. There are obviously very differing regulations laid down in the production, packaging and handling of food for human consumption as against food for animal or fish consumption. As far as we are concerned, there is nothing in the product which would be harmful if consumed by a human but we cannot <u>recommend</u> it since it was not produced for this purpose nor has it passed the stringent tests to pronounce it fit for human consumption.

We are sorry that we cannot be more helpful.

Yours sincerely

Julie Parker
<u>Customer Services Administrator</u>

The Elms
Wenter Road
New Mills
High Peak
Derbyshire

Julie Parker
Interpet Ltd   23rd May
Vincent Lane
Dorking
Surrey
RH4 3YX

Dear Julie Parker

Thank you for your letter of 20th May.

Henry continues to enjoy Floating Food Hoops mixed in with his Kellogg's Honey Nut Loops. My wife swears he is developing scales on his lower left leg, but it's just a particularly bad case of athlete's foot if you ask me.

Thank you for all your help.

Yours sincerely

T Ravenscroft (Mr)

The Elms
Wenter Road
New Mills
High Peak
Derbyshire

9th April

Kellogg's Ltd
Talbot Road
Manchester
M16 0PU

Dear Kellogg's

I attach a letter I recently sent to Interpet, which I would like you to read before continuing.

It occurred to me that if my son Henry preferred Floating Food Hoops to your Honey Nut Loops, then my collection of Japanese Koi fish might prefer Honey Nut Loops to Floating Food Hoops. I decided to find out, for if this proved to be the case, I could save myself quite a bit of money, Floating Food Hoops being five times as expensive as Honey Nut Loops. Sadly, the experiment was not a success. Not only did most of the Koi shun the Honey Nut Loops completely, but the only one that ate them died the following day.

The exercise wasn't a complete disaster, however, as my wife and I had the Koi grilled for supper with some oven chips, and very nice it was too, but as it had cost me over £200 not so long ago, it isn't a meal I want to eat too often.

Why the fish died is something of a mystery. I have looked at the list of ingredients on the Honey Nut Loops packet and they aren't a great deal different to the ingredients in Floating Food Hoops. Where they do differ is that you use niacin and folic acid. Could it be either of these two substances that caused the demise of my Koi?

Yours faithfully

T Ravenscroft (Mr)

The Elms
Wenter Road
New Mills
High Peak
Derbyshire

Cadbury Ltd
Bournville   12th April
Birmingham
B30 2LU

Dear Cadbury

Might I congratulate you on the position you have taken with
regard to product placement, since taking on the mantle of
Coronation Street's sponsor. It would have been all too easy for
you to put pressure on the programme's producers to include
in each episode gratuitous close-ups of your products, but I
can honestly say I have yet to see so much as a Chocolate
Button on my favourite soap! Given the more liberal attitude
to sex taken by the producers of *Coronation Street* nowadays, it
would have been all too easy to feature shots of Deirdre
nibbling a Milk Flake or Liz sucking a Walnut Whip, but no,
your restraint has been admirable. I take my hat off to you.

Yours faithfully

T Ravenscroft (Mr)

The first name in chocolate

CADBURY LTD.

PO BOX 12
BOURNVILLE
BIRMINGHAM B30 2LU

Our ref; L17/CD/SF

22nd April

Mr T Ravenscroft
The Elms
Wenter Road
New Mills
High Peak
Derbyshire

Dear Mr Ravenscroft,

Thank you for your letter dated 12th April concerning the Cadbury sponsorship of Coronation Street.

I thank you for your kind words concerning our sponsorship, as you correctly state it would be quite improper of us to influence the programme in any way, be it having our products included, or trying to influence the story lines of the show.

I note however that you say it would be easy to feature shots of a Flake or a Walnut Whip, but I can assure you that as we do not produce Walnut Whip that is one product we would certainly be trying not to get featured!

Once again thank you for taking the trouble to write to us.

Yours sincerely,

Carol Dunseith
Consumer Services Manager

The Elms
Wenter Road
New Mills
High Peak
Derbyshire

24th April

Your ref L17/CD/SF

Carol Dunseith
Cadbury Ltd
PO Box 12
Bournville
Birmingham
B30 2LU

Dear Carol Dunseith

It's Sod's Law, isn't it? No sooner do I congratulate you on your restraint than you go and blot your copybook. I refer of course to last Monday's episode of *Coronation Street* when Emily was to be seen looking longingly at a Mars Bar in the Corner Shop. Let's hope this was just a temporary lapse!

My apologies for thinking that you make Walnut Whips. They are certainly good enough to be made by Cadbury's. Who makes them?

Yours sincerely

T Ravenscroft (Mr)

CADBURY LTD.

THE CHOCOLATE. THE TASTE.

PO BOX 12
BOURNVILLE
BIRMINGHAM B30 2LU

29 April

Mr T Ravenscroft
The Elms
Wenter Road
New Mills
High Peak
Derbyshire

Our Ref:- 0316231B JAP

Dear Mr Ravenscroft,

Thank you for your letter dated 24th April concerning Cadbury products on Coronation Street.

I was sorry to learn that you feel we have now blotted our copybook because Emily looked longingly at a Mars Bar in one episode last week. Cadbury do not produce Mars Bars these are made by Mars. But now that a Mars Bar has been featured, I do hope you will think it is only fair if one of our products does appear in the future!

In answer to your question concerning Walnut Whips these are made by Nestle. I note you think they are good enough to be made by Cadbury's, but I don't think their chocolate is as nice as ours but I would say that wouldn't I!

Thank you for writing to us.

Yours sincerely

Carol Dunseith
Consumer Services Manager

The Elms
Wenter Road
New Mills
High Peak
Derbyshire

Your ref 0336231B JAP

2nd May

Carol Dunseith
Cadbury Ltd
PO Box 12
Bournville
Birmingham
B30 2LU

Dear Carol Dunseith

Thank you for your letter of 29th April.

You are right, it would only be fair if one of your products were to appear in a future episode of *Coronation Street*. I don't know whether or not you have any influence with the scriptwriters, but a scene with Norris balancing Smarties on Rita's nipples, then flicking them off into a Cadbury's Chocolate Easter Egg held by Jack Duckworth might go down well. What do you think?

Yours sincerely

T Ravenscroft (Mr)

The Elms
Wenter Road
New Mills
High Peak
Derbyshire

Batchelors Foods
Croydon   15th April
CR9 1JQ

Dear Batchelors Foods

I have just used one of your Delicately Flavoured Rice packets, and very nice it was too. I just wish there had been more of it. In fact, I expected there to be more of it, as it clearly stated on the packet '3 to 4 servings'. To whom do these servings relate exactly, sparrows?

If this seems facetious it certainly isn't meant to be, because after following your cooking instructions, and dividing the cooked rice into four, I can honestly say that each of the four portions was a good deal smaller than the portions of rice I saw being doled out to the prisoners of war in the film *The Bridge on the River Kwai*. In fact, if they'd had to survive on your portions of Delicately Flavoured Rice, there's a good chance they would still be building the bridge, Alec Guinness or no Alec Guinness.

Is it possible I got a faulty packet?

Yours faithfully

T Ravenscroft (Mr)

Brooke House
Manor Royal
Crawley
West Sussex
RH10 2RQ

April 21   REF 0061055A

Mr T Ravenscroft
The Elms
Wenter Road
New Mills
High Peak
Derbyshire

Dear Mr Ravenscroft,

We regret to learn of your recent experience
with a packet of Batchelors Delicately Flavoured
Rice.

We continuously monitor our quality control
procedures to ensure that we achieve
consistently high levels of product quality and
the most meticulous care is taken to enable you
to enjoy our products in perfect condition. It
is therefore particularly disappointing to us
that in this instance our product failed to give
you complete satisfaction.

We would stress that this product is, of course,
intended as an accompaniment to a meal. Before
any new products are launched by us on a
national scale, they are first test marketed in
one or two areas for a long period of time. In
this way we are able to collect all kinds of
consumer reaction to the product, the type and
design of packaging and, of course, quantities,
texture and taste.

We sincerely regret that despite the precautions undertaken you have had cause to bring this matter to our attention. We wish to express our sincere apologies for the inconvenience caused from this purchase and hope that you will accept the reimbursement enclosed as a goodwill gesture from our part. We trust that you will find all future purchases to your satisfaction.

Yours sincerely

Jayne Pratt (Mrs)
Consumer Services Manager

Enclosure(s)
    4 x Batchelors 50p Voucher

The Elms
Wenter Road
New Mills
High Peak
Derbyshire

Uncle Ben's
Master Foods UK   16th April
King's Lynn
PE30 4JE

Dear Uncle Ben

I have just dined on a jar of your Sweet and Sour Sauce, which I had with chicken and a rather frugal portion of Batchelor's Delicately Flavoured Rice. (I should have taken the advice on your label and used Uncle Ben's Long Grain Rice instead!)

It is an irony then that it is something on your label about which I feel I must take you to task. However, before I start beefing, I would like to make it quite clear that the taste of your Sweet and Sour Sauce is excellent, quite the best I have ever tasted outside a Chinese restaurant, and a good deal better than inside most of them! No, my niggle concerns your use of the words 'A sweet and sour sauce with a selection of crispy vegetables'. Now, I won't deny that the vegetables in question could have been crispy at some time in their career, but they certainly weren't very crispy when they reached my bowl and chopsticks. 'Soggy' would be a more apt description of their condition.

But then, how could they be crispy? Let's face it, after lying in sweet and sour sauce for any length of time it would take a bamboo pole all its time to remain crispy, never mind a bamboo shoot. I realise of course that you can't very well print 'A sweet and sour sauce with a selection of soggy vegetables' on your label, as this would no doubt put the customers off, and you have to make a living, but why not dispense with the description altogether? I am sure it does little to influence the customer's choice, and it would make an honest company out of you.

Otherwise, keep up the good work.

Yours faithfully

T Ravenscroft (Mr)

Master Foods

A DIVISION OF MARS UK LTD

HANSA ROAD   KING'S LYNN   NORFOLK   PE30 4JE

Mr T Ravenscroft   April 21
The Elms
Wenter Road
New Mills
High Peak
Derbyshire

Dear Mr Ravenscroft,

We were concerned to receive your letter advising us of your
disappointment with your recent purchase of Uncle Ben's Sweet
& Sour With Vegetables.

We take great care in the development of our products to ensure that
they meet the needs of the consumer and during the manufacture of our
products we insist on a high level of quality for raw materials and in-plant
processing.

We introduced this product into the market after conducting product and
consumer research to ensure that as responsible food manufacturers the
product was acceptable to our customers.

We do take notice of what our customers have to say, and have accordingly
forwarded your comments on to our Marketing and R&D colleagues for
consideration.

We apologise for the inconvenience this has caused, and enclose
compensation which we hope will make amends for your disappointment.

Yours sincerely,
MASTER FOODS

Nancy Livingstone
CONSUMER SERVICES

The Elms
Wenter Road
New Mills
High Peak
Derbyshire

Nancy Livingstone
Master Foods
Hansa Road
King's Lynn
Norfolk
PE30 4JE

22nd April

Dear Nancy Livingstone

You seem to have got the wrong idea entirely from my letter.

I certainly wasn't disappointed with Uncle Ben's Sweet and Sour Sauce, far from it. No, the point I was making is that your 'selection of crispy vegetables' weren't crispy, but nor could they be, so why not dispense with this description and make an honest company of yourself? Remember the words of Robert Maxwell – 'An honest company is a happy company.'

I am pleased you have passed on my comments to your Marketing and R&D colleagues, and will be most interested in what they have to say. Should I contact them direct or can I leave it to you to pass on their observations to me?

Yours sincerely

T Ravenscroft (Mr)

The Elms
Wenter Road
New Mills
High Peak
Derbyshire

Aunt Bessie's
Tryton Foods
Trinity Street   17th April
Hull
HU3 1EY

Dear Aunt Bessie

I have just had the misfortune to try one of your Yorkshire Pudding Beef Dinners. I say misfortune, because what might have been an excellent meal was spoiled by the lack of adequate heating instructions on the packet. Your instructions clearly state: 'Remove carton and film wrapping, leaving paper disc on meal, and place on a suitable plate.' As my wife quite rightly pointed out, at no stage in the subsequent instructions is one told to remove the paper disc.

Now you might argue that it would only be common sense to remove the paper disc once the meal is heated through, but unfortunately common sense is not a commodity which my wife has an abundance of – I married her for her looks – so consequently she served up the meal to me with the paper disc still between the Yorkshire Pudding Dinner and the plate. Eating paper, even along with a Yorkshire Pudding Dinner, is not a pleasant experience. Whether or not it was eating the paper disc which gave me diarrhoea the following day I'm not sure – if I was sure, this letter would be coming from my solicitor, not me – but what I am sure of is that it was an altogether unpleasant and unnecessary experience. This can't be the first time it has happened, and to ensure that it doesn't happen again, I suggest that you amend the instructions on your packet accordingly.

Yours faithfully

T Ravenscroft (Mr)

Trinity Street, Hull, HU3 1EY

Our Ref 662/JB/MG/97

23 April

Mr T Ravenscroft
The Elms
Wenter Road
New Mills
High Peak
Derbyshire

Dear Mr Ravenscroft   WITHOUT PREJUDICE

Thank you for your letter of 17 April which we have read with interest.

We sell approximately 250,000 units annually of Beef Dinner (and the same of Chicken Dinner) and you may be surprised to know that your letter is the first of its kind.

You state in your letter that the paper was 'between the plate and the pudding', I am intrigued to know whether it was also served to you upside down as the paper covers and protects the pudding contents!

However, we are sorry to hear that the product was served to you in an uncustomary fashion, which I am sure was in no way beneficial to its eating quality.

We hope the enclosed voucher to the value of £3.00 will help persuade you that Aunt Bessie's products can indeed be most enjoyable.

Yours sincerely

JACKY BOWES
Technical Controller
Enc

The Elms
Wenter Road
New Mills
High Peak
Derbyshire

Your ref 662/JB/MG/97

28th April

Jacky Bowes
Tryton Foods
Trinity Street
Hull
HU3 1EY

Dear Jacky Bowes

Thank you for your letter of 23rd April.

I suppose on reflection that, as you have intimated, the Beef Dinner must have been served up to me upside down. This would not come as a surprise to you, nor would the fact that it is apparently the first time it has ever happened despite your selling 250,000 units annually, if you had been exposed to the culinary expertise of my wife for any length of time. We are talking here of a woman who once roasted an undrawn chicken. She had also contrived to stuff the fowl with sage and onion stuffing, though don't ask me how. I am quite confident that without too much effort she could burn water.

With your vouchers I tried Aunt Bessie's Toad In The Hole, taking the precaution of heating it up myself. It was very nice, although I would have preferred a little more Toad and a bit less Hole. Your portion-control manager didn't used to work for Batchelors, did he?

Yours sincerely

T Ravenscroft (Mr)

The Elms
Wenter Road
New Mills
High Peak
Derbyshire

Birds Eye Wall's Ltd
Walton-on-Thames   20th April
Surrey
KT12 1NT

Dear Birds Eye Wall's

I have long been a fan of your Boil-in-the-bag Kipper Fillets and have them for breakfast every day when I am at home. However, I have to spend a good deal of my time on the Continent on business. With a little effort, it is sometimes possible to buy fresh kippers whilst abroad, but I have as yet never been able to buy your Boil-in-the-bag Kipper Fillets, which I much prefer.

In an effort to simulate the taste, I have tried boiling a plastic bag in the pan along with the fresh kippers, in the hope they would take on the unique boil-in-the-bag flavour, but sadly the kippers have always remained resolutely unboiled-in-the-bag-like. With this in mind, I was wondering if you could advise me on anything else I could try in my efforts to get fresh kippers to taste like yours?

I look forward to hearing from you.

Yours faithfully

T Ravenscroft (Mr)

BIRDS EYE WALL'S

Working Together For The Best

CONSUMER
SERVICES

Birds Eye Wall's Limited, Station Avenue, Walton on Thames, Surrey KT12 1NT.

Mr T Ravenscroft
The Elms
Wenter Road
New Mills
High Peak
Derbyshire

14 May

Dear Mr Ravenscroft,

Thank you for your letter about our boil-in-bag kippers. As you have discovered, we do not export these to anywhere in Europe; I think the whole concept is essentially British.

The result which you get from the Birds Eye product is not actually imparted by the plastic itself and this would account for the fact that you cannot get such a good result if you add a plastic bag to the water when you cook kippers abroad. The flavour and succulence of these kippers is largely due to the fact that they are packed into the sealed bag (together with butter pat) and then quick frozen immediately after curing. The quick freezing ensures that the fish is kept really fresh tasting, and this taste is preserved by the fact that nothing is lost in the water and steam which is involved in boiling or poaching in an open pan.

You do not say whether the kippers you buy abroad are ready frozen, but I suspect that they are not. So it is not possible from this point of view to simulate the flavour. But it is possible to buy very strong, boilable plastic bags in which you can create your own boil-in-bag dishes. You simply put the raw – frozen or unfrozen – fish or meat into the bag, adding butter or other seasoning and excluding as much air as you can, then secure the neck of the bag with a strong wire tie or a heat sealer. It can then be boiled in the normal way. But sadly even this would not guarantee that you will get the unique Birds Eye effect because obviously the quality of the fish itself is likely to be variable.

I hope this is helpful.

Yours sincerely,

LINDA BELL

Assistant Consumer Services Manager

The Elms
Wenter Road
New Mills
High Peak
Derbyshire

Linda Bell
Birds Eye Wall's Ltd   21st May
Station Avenue
Walton-on-Thames
Surrey
KT12 1NT

Dear Linda Bell

Thank you for your letter of 14th May.

I took your advice and made myself some do-it-yourself boil-in-the-bag kippers. I bought some kippers from my local fishmonger, who assured me that they were of the finest quality, put them in a strong plastic bag with a generous pat of Lurpak, excluded all the air, then sealed them with my wife's steam iron. (If I do any more I will have to think of something else, because after using the iron the following day, my wife complained her leotard smelt of fish.)

I am afraid the result was a bit of a disappointment, as the kippers did not reach your high standard. However, I then tried an experiment, boiling a pair of kippers, which I had purchased at the same time, in one of your boil-in-the-bag plastic bags. These kippers tasted exactly the same as yours! It wasn't just my imagination either, because in order to test my findings, I then boiled two Aunt Bessie's Individual Yorkshire Puddings, one in an ordinary plastic bag and one in one of your plastic bags, and the one boiled in your plastic bag tasted far superior.

It would appear then that your plastic bags have a greater influence on the taste of your kippers than you give them credit for. With this in mind, I was wondering if I could purchase a quantity of them from you?

Yours sincerely

T Ravenscroft (Mr)

BIRDS EYE WALL'S

Working Together For The Best

CONSUMER SERVICES

Birds Eye Wall's Limited, Station Avenue,
Walton-on-Thames, Surrey KT12 1NT.

Mr T Ravenscroft
The Elms
Wenter Road
New Mills
High Peak
Derbyshire

11 June

Dear Mr Ravenscroft,

Thank you for your further letter about getting the authentic boil-in-bag taste with your kippers. I am sorry that my suggestions did not give you a satisfactory result.

I very much regret that we are not able to supply you with some of these bags. Quite apart from anything else, it would be impossible for us to donate any items of packaging, not so much because of its value but because our production plants simply do not have the human resource which would be needed to extract these items from pallets, pack them up, address and despatch them on a regular basis. But in any case the bags are not preformed; we buy all this type of polythene packaging on a roll and the machine which packs the products also shapes and seals the bags.

I am sorry to disappoint you. I fear you will have to keep on buying the Birds Eye brand for complete satisfaction.

Yours sincerely,

LINDA BELL
Assistant Consumer Services Manager

The Elms
Wenter Road
New Mills
High Peak
Derbyshire

Linda Bell
Birds Eye Wall's Ltd   17th June
Station Avenue
Walton-on-Thames
Surrey
KT12 1NT

Dear Linda Bell

Thank you for your letter of 11th June. However, you don't shake off a boil-in-the-bag kipper fan as easily as that! Regarding your point about your inability to supply me on a regular basis, there would be no need for you to do this as I will quite happily take a lifetime's supply in one go. I have worked out my requirements and, assuming that I live to be eighty (which I am sure to do if I continue to eat Birds Eye Boil-in-the-bag Kipper Fillets!), I will need a roll of polythene 2,125 metres long by one metre wide.

Fortunately, I will be in the Walton-on-Thames area on the 1st of August, so I will pop into your factory to pick it up. In the meantime, if you could let me know the cost, I will put you a cheque in the post.

Yours sincerely

T Ravenscroft (Mr)

BIRDS EYE WALL'S

Working Together For The Best

CONSUMER
SERVICES

Birds Eye Wall's Limited, Station Avenue,
Walton-on-Thames, Surrey KT12 1NT.

07 July

Mr T Ravenscroft
The Elms
Wenter Road
New Mills
High Peak
Derbyshire

Dear Mr Ravenscroft,

Thank you for your further letter on the subject of boil-in-bag kippers. I am very sorry that we are not able to help you by supplying some of the material. We receive a number of requests for packaging – tubs, plates, foil trays and so on – but unfortunately do not have the mechanisms by which we can respond to these requests.

Incidentally, the address here at Walton-on-Thames is an office, not a factory, so there is no stock of any packaging material held here.

Please accept our apologies once again.

Yours sincerely

Linda Bell
Assistant Consumer Services Manager

The Elms
Wenter Road
New Mills
High Peak
Derbyshire

Linda Bell
Birds Eye Wall's Ltd   10th July
Station Avenue
Walton-on-Thames
Surrey
KT12 1NT

Dear Linda Spoilsport Bell

I really expected better from a company whose products I buy at least five times a week. I will never eat Birds Eye Boil-in-the-bag Kipper Fillets again!

Yours sincerely

T Ravenscroft (Mr)

The Elms
Wenter Road
New Mills
High Peak
Derbyshire

Bernard Matthews Foods Ltd
Norwich   21st April
Norfolk
NR9 5QD

Dear Bernard Matthews

Very surprisingly, I have a complaint to make about your
Willy Whales. I say surprisingly because, although I am not
personally familiar with your turkey products, preferring my
turkey only at Christmas and with traditional chestnut stuffing
and oven chips, my three children absolutely love them.

The complaint comes from my middle son Henry, who
reports that your Willy Whales taste fishy. Now it must be
admitted that Henry has not the most discerning of palates, far
too much junk food passes his lips for him to be able to claim
that, but I tried a bite of a Willy Whale myself and I must say
I agree with him.

I realise of course that your turkeys are fed fish products, and
that this can lead to your turkey meat usually tasting a bit on
the fishy side, but the turkey meat in your Willy Whales was
extremely fishy indeed. Maybe you could offer up an
explanation for this?

Yours faithfully

T Ravenscroft (Mr)

Mr T Ravenscroft   7th May
The Elms   Ref. No. BM9710099-1
Wenter Road
New Mills
High Peak
Derbyshire

Dear Mr Ravenscroft,

Thank you for your letter concerning a pack of
Willy Whales you recently purchased. We are
indeed sorry that it was necessary for you to
contact us and we are pleased to be given the
opportunity to resolve the matter.

Willy Whales are one of the products from our
fish range and as the packaging states are
"crunchy golden whale shapes made from selected
flaked white fish". However, if your son was
expecting a turkey product, we can certainly
appreciate his concern.

In the circumstances we have pleasure in
enclosing our cheque for £10.00 and we feel
certain you will receive every satisfaction
from our products in the future.

Yours sincerely,
for BERNARD MATTHEWS FOODS LTD.

ANNE PETERS
SENIOR CONSUMER RELATIONS ASSISTANT

The Elms
Wenter Road
New Mills
High Peak
Derbyshire

15th May

Your ref BM9710099-1

Anne Peters
Bernard Matthews Foods Ltd
Great Witching
Norwich
Norfolk
NR9 5QD

Dear Anne Peters

Thank you for your letter of 7th May, and the cheque for £10.00. At first I was going to return it, as I don't normally accept charity. However, on this occasion I decided to keep it as compensation for a bad experience I had the only time I ever tried one of your Lamb Roasts.

Turning to the matter of your Willy Whales, it would seem that I owe you an apology. My wife has since bought another packet and you are quite right, the packet does state that they are 'crunchy golden whale shapes'.

I must say I feel you are being a bit ambitious in likening them to a whale, though, because if Willy Whales are indeed whale-shaped, then the whale in question belongs to a species of whale that I have never come across. In fact, to my eyes your Willy Whales are just as likely to be taken for willies as they are for whales. It is quite amazing how one's opinion can change once in possession of all the facts, isn't it? Before I received your letter, I thought that Willy Whales were turkey pieces that tasted a bit like fish. However, now that I know they are made of fish, my perception of them is completely different, because I can categorically say that they are fish pieces that taste a bit like turkey. Do you think this could be because you deep-fry them in the same fat in which you fry your turkey products?

Yours sincerely

T Ravenscroft (Mr)

The Elms
Wenter Road
New Mills
High Peak
Derbyshire

Bisto Foods
Middlewich
Cheshire
CW10 0HD

15th May

Dear Bisto Foods

Last week, my wife inadvertently put a pair of my middle son Henry's trousers into a bucket of water to soak, prior to washing them. It later transpired that there was a packet of your Bisto Gravy Granules in one of the pockets. Unfortunately, there were also six pairs of my white underpants in the bucket and, after being soaked overnight, they became brown underpants. (Why on earth my wife finds it necessary to soak my underpants prior to washing them is a mystery that only she knows the answer to.) However, after being put through the washer my underpants more or less reverted back to white, but had taken on a distinct smell of gravy. Now I quite like the smell of gravy, but not on my underpants, and yesterday on my walk from the railway station a dog followed me all the way home.

The thing is, I'm sure that your workers' clothes must become permeated with the smell of Bisto Gravy Granules and take on the similar 'Bisto Gravy' smell of my underpants, so I was wondering if you could ask them how they get rid of the smell, and let me know?

I look forward to hearing from you.

Yours faithfully

T Ravenscroft (Mr)

BISTO FOODS

Booth Lane, Middlewich, Cheshire, CW10 0HH

21st May

Mr T Ravenscroft
The Elms
Wenter Road
New Mills
High Peak
Derbyshire

Dear Mr Ravenscroft,

Thank you for your recent letter regarding an enquiry about our product Bisto Gravy Granules.

We were most interested in your letter due to the unusual nature of the information you required.

We have enquired with the industrial laundry that launder our protective workwear and they have assured us that normal domestic washing soap or detergents and washing machines will remove any of the food flavours and colours used in our products.

Yours sincerely,

J K HANSON
CONSUMER SERVICES

Bisto Foods Limited Registered in England No 2473082
Registered Office: East Putney House, 84 Upper Richmond Road, London SW15 2ST

The Elms
Wenter Road
New Mills
High Peak
Derbyshire

J K Hanson
Bisto Foods
Booth Lane
Middlewich
Cheshire
CW10 0HD

27th May

Dear J K Hanson

Since writing to you on 15th May, something quite remarkable has happened. It's rather personal, so I would appreciate it if you would keep it to yourself. The thing is, the day after writing to you, my wife and I made love, it being Saturday, after *Match of the Day*. My wife, although very appreciative, has up to now always been a silent lover, but her beauty more than makes up for her lack of vocal enthusiasm. However, on this occasion, and but a few seconds into the act, she emitted a quite loud and appreciative 'Aaaaaah'. This of course pleased me immensely. My joy was short-lived, however, because almost immediately afterwards, she followed the 'Aaaaaah' with a cry of 'Bisto!'

What had apparently happened was that she had caught a whiff of my Bisto-impregnated underpants. Initially, I was a little put out to say the least, what with my efforts at love-making coming second in the appreciation stakes to a jar of gravy granules, but we carried on and it turned out to be the most satisfying bout of sex we have had in our entire married life.

Since then, I have worn Bisto-flavoured underpants to bed every night, and our sex life has been utterly transformed.

Rather than try to remove the smell of Bisto from my underpants, I now ensure that they are always given a good soaking in 'Bisto water' prior to being washed. (Despite what you say in your letter about normal domestic washing soap removing the smell, it does tend to linger.)

Why the smell of Bisto turns my wife on I neither know nor care. Maybe it is the 'animal' smell of it. I would be interested to know if you have ever come across this sort of thing before, as I am considering using it as the subject of a speech I will soon be giving to the New Mills Young Mothers Group.

Yours sincerely

T Ravenscroft (Mr)

The Elms
Wenter Road
New Mills
High Peak
Derbyshire

G Costa and Co Ltd
Aylesford   26th April
Kent
ME20 7NA

Dear G Costa

My wife is forever making disparaging remarks about my breath
and pointedly leaving Clorets around the house, so you can
imagine my delight when I read on a can of your Blue Dragon
Water Chestnuts that they 'are considered "yin", and cooling,
and are thought to sweeten the breath'. Here we go, I said to
myself, cool sweet breath, just the thing to quieten her.

The following day, I stir-fried the whole of the contents of the
can with some diced squid, about half-a-dozen cloves of garlic,
four slices of root ginger, and a dessertspoonful of five-spice
powder, and ate the lot with some Batchelors Aromatic Rice.
Then, confident in the knowledge that my breath would pass
muster, I walked up to my wife and planted a smacker full on her
lips. She kicked me! At a loss as to her behaviour, I asked her
why. She told me I smelled like a drain.

In view of the claim on your can that my breath would be cool
and sweet after eating your water chestnuts, would you care to
explain this?

Yours faithfully

T Ravenscroft (Mr)

The World's Finest Foods

G. COSTA & COMPANY LIMITED
AYLESFORD, KENT ME20 7NA

Ref: JD

12th May

Mr T Ravenscroft
The Elms
Wenter Road
New Mills
High Peak
Derbyshire

Dear Mr Ravenscroft,

Re: Blue Dragon Water Chestnuts

Thank you for your letter of 26th April regarding the above product.

We appreciate your comments regarding the breath freshening aspect of this vegetable, however, as with any food if it is mixed with other ingredients, especially those with strong flavour such as garlic, unfortunately the effect is not the same! We have also scoured our stock to locate a label claiming these freshening qualities.

Thank you for purchasing Blue Dragon.

Yours sincerely,
for G COSTA & CO LTD

Joanne Dann
Consumer Relations Department

Your ref JD

The Elms
Wenter Road
New Mills
High Peak
Derbyshire

Joanne Dann
G Costa and Co Ltd
Aylesford
Kent
ME20 7NA

15th May

Dear Joanne Dann

If you have in fact scoured your stock to locate on the label the claim that your Blue Dragon Water Chestnuts have freshening qualities, then all I can say is you need a new scourer.

I attach, for your information, a label which clearly claims such qualities, and I consider that if you make such claims, you should be prepared to stand by them. Furthermore, your failing to point out on your label that if your water chestnuts are mixed with other ingredients then their power to sweeten the breath is negated, which resulted in my suffering a badly bruised shin, is nothing less than negligence. Unless you want to risk others meeting the same fate, I would seriously consider a major label rethink if I were you.

I had to buy another can of your water chestnuts in order to obtain a label, so I expect you to reimburse me with the cost.

Yours sincerely

T Ravenscroft (Mr)

The World's Finest Foods

G. COSTA & COMPANY LIMITED
AYLESFORD, KENT ME20 7NA

Ref: JD

22nd May

Mr T Ravenscroft
The Elms
Wenter Road
New Mills
High Peak
Derbyshire

Dear Mr Ravenscroft,

Re: Blue Dragon Water Chestnuts

Thank you for your letter of 15th May regarding the above.

I appreciate your comments regarding our labelling and can confirm that the new labels are indeed not quite the same as the one you have supplied to us.

As requested, please find enclosed a postal order for £1.00 in respect of the tin of Water Chestnuts purchased for its label.

Yours sincerely,
for G COSTA & CO LTD

Joanne Dann
Consumer Relations Department

The Elms
Wenter Road
New Mills
High Peak
Derbyshire

Joanne Dann
G Costa and Co Ltd   28th May
Aylesford
Kent
ME20 7NA

Dear Joanne Dann

Thank you for your letter of 22nd May.

I have visited several supermarkets and scoured the labels of your Blue Dragon Water Chestnuts, but have found no evidence whatsoever of any change in the wording on them. I have also scoured the envelope of your letter and found no evidence of a £1.00 postal order! Perhaps the inefficient employee who scoured your stock for evidence of your claiming freshening qualities for your water chestnuts was the same person who was responsible for putting the postal order in the envelope?

Would you now be good enough to send me one of your new labels, so that I can check if the new wording is satisfactory, along with a postal order for £1.20 to cover the postal order that you claim to have already sent but haven't, plus the 32 pence it is going to cost me to send this additional letter.

Yours sincerely

T Ravenscroft (Mr)

The World's Finest Foods

G. COSTA & COMPANY LIMITED
AYLESFORD, KENT ME20 7NA

Ref: ES

11 June

Mr T Ravenscroft
The Elms
Wenter Road
New Mills
High Peak
Derbyshire

Dear Mr Ravenscroft,

Re: Blue Dragon Water Chestnuts

We acknowledge receipt of your letter dated 28 May and apologise that the Postal Order was omitted from our letter of 22 May. Accordingly we enclose a Postal Order for £2.00 and trust you will find this satisfactory.

Yours sincerely,
for G COSTA & CO LTD

Elizabeth Sims
Consumer Relations Department

Enc

The Elms
Wenter Road
New Mills
High Peak
Derbyshire

27th April

Taylors of Harrogate
Yorkshire Tea
Pagoda House
Prospect Road
Harrogate
North Yorkshire
HG2 7NX

Dear Taylors of Harrogate

Although I have always lived quite close to Yorkshire, I must confess that I have never felt the desire to visit the White Rose county. Maybe this is because the names of some of the towns and villages sound so uninviting – Greaseborough, Slaithwaite and Grewelthorpe spring readily to mind, but no doubt I could find a Snotborough if I tried hard enough. Probably by the time God got to Yorkshire He must have run out of attractive names and you got the barrel-scrapings, as it were. However, and to get to the point, I have recently been introduced to the delights of 'Yorkshire Tea', which in turn has led to me deciding to visit your county in the not too distant future. If the climate in Yorkshire is hot enough to grow tea, then clearly I have been missing something! During my stay, I would like very much to visit your tea plantations. Would this be possible?

I look forward to hearing from you.

Yours faithfully

T Ravenscroft (Mr)

TAYLORS
of HARROGATE · EST 1886
Tea Blenders & Coffee Roasters

Taylors of Harrogate, Pagoda House, Prospect Road, Harrogate, North Yorkshire HG2 7NX

1st May

Dear Mr Ravencroft,

Thank you for your recent letter and kind comments about Yorkshire Tea. We always enjoy reading letters from our Yorkshire Tea customers and we really do appreciate the time and trouble taken to write. We were particularly delighted to read that you were thinking of visiting Yorkshire for the first time thanks to your enjoyment of our tea!

We are still a small family business with over a hundred years' experience of buying and blending tea. Our Tea Buyer visits tea estates around the world, selecting only the very best tea for our blends. This helps to give Yorkshire Tea its rich refreshing flavour. However it does mean that you would have to travel much further afield than Yorkshire to visit tea plantations.

Thank you once again for your letter and your interest in our business. Please find enclosed a sample of Yorkshire Tea so that you can enjoy your next cup with our compliments.

Yours sincerely

Katy Squire
Assistant PR & Promotions Manager

Mr T Ravenscroft
The Elms
Wenter Road
New Mills
High Peak
Derbyshire

Bettys & Taylors of Harrogate Ltd Registered Number 543821 England
Registered Office 1 Parliament Street Harrogate HG1 2QU

The Elms
Wenter Road
New Mills
High Peak
Derbyshire

Katy Squire   6th May
Taylors of Harrogate
Yorkshire Tea
Pagoda House
Prospect Road
Harrogate
North Yorkshire
HG2 7NX

Dear Katy Squire

Thank you for your letter of 1st May and the sample of
Yorkshire Tea. I used it to make a pot of tea, which I shared
with the Vicar when he called round to bless my eldest son
Marcus's new iguana, and he was converted. (To Yorkshire Tea,
that is, he was already converted to the Church of England
faith, naturally.)

I was both surprised and disappointed to learn that the tea that
goes into Yorkshire Tea isn't grown in Yorkshire. It's none of
my business of course, but aren't you breaking the Trades
Description Act or something by calling it Yorkshire Tea?

Yours sincerely

T Ravenscroft (Mr)

TAYLORS
of HARROGATE · EST 1886
Tea Blenders & Coffee Roasters

Taylors of Harrogate, Pagoda House, Prospect Road, Harrogate, North Yorkshire HG2 7NX

8th May

Dear Mr Ravencroft,

Thank you for your recent letter. We were delighted to read that you have converted your Vicar to Yorkshire Tea!

Thank you also for your enquiry regarding the name of Yorkshire Tea. We would love to be able to grow tea here in Harrogate although sadly the climatic conditions are far from ideal! Instead our Tea Buyer visits tea estates and tea gardens around the world searching for fine quality teas to use in our blends.

Taylors of Harrogate was founded in 1886 and we remain very proud of our Yorkshire heritage. Still today all our teas are blended and packed in Harrogate and for this reason our rich, refreshing blend is called Yorkshire Tea. The name is registered and trade marked.

Thank you once again for your interest in our business and we do hope you will continue to enjoy drinking Yorkshire Tea.

Yours sincerely

Katy Squire
Assistant PR & Promotions Manager

Mr T Ravenscroft
The Elms
Wenter Road
New Mills
High Peak
Derbyshire

Bettys & Taylors of Harrogate Ltd Registered Number 543821 England
Registered Office 1 Parliament Street Harrogate HG1 2QU

The Elms
Wenter Road
New Mills
High Peak
Derbyshire

Katy Squire
Taylors of Harrogate   21st May
Yorkshire Tea
Pagoda House
Prospect Road
Harrogate
North Yorkshire
HG2 7NX

Dear Katy Squire

Hello again! Just a line to let you know that last weekend my wife and I visited the Yorkshire Dales, staying in Wharfedale. What a lovely part of the country! And such nice people.

The only disappointment apart from the unseasonable weather was with the Yorkshire Tea which we drank whilst in Yorkshire. For some reason it didn't taste nearly so good as it does here in Derbyshire. As a matter of fact it wasn't all that easy to come by either, and I had to get the landlady at the guest house where we were staying to buy in some Yorkshire Tea specially, as she 'Allus got that tea what t'monkeys advertise on t'telly as it were a bloody seet tastier', as she charmingly put it. I wonder if this could have something to do with the water? I ask this because the domestic water supply in the High Peak is excellent, and far superior to the water that emerged through our tap in Grassington. In fact, my wife refused point blank to drink Grassington tap water and I had to go all the way to Skipton to get her a bottle of Perrier, but then she's always been a bit squeamish about what she'll put in her mouth ever since our honeymoon (when she got drunk on Cherry B).

You remember the Vicar I introduced to Yorkshire Tea? The other day he ran off with a lady bellringer, but I doubt it was anything to do with drinking your tea.

Yours sincerely

T Ravenscroft (Mr)

END OF CORRESPONDENCE

The Elms
Wenter Road
New Mills
High Peak
Derbyshire

HP Foods
Tower Road
Aston Cross
Birmingham
B6 5AB

30th April

Dear HP Foods

Being something of a gourmet, I make a point of watching as many television cookery programmes as time allows. However, despite seeing all that the Two Fat Ladies had to offer, and sitting through Rick Stein, Gary Rhodes, Raymond Blanc, Jamie Oliver, countless series of Delia Smith, and Floyd on France, Italy, Spain, Australia and God knows where else, I have yet to see a single TV chef use HP Sauce, whether included in the recipe or on the finished dish.

I find this quite amazing, as a generous helping of your excellent condiment will improve any dish. I have found that three tablespoonfuls added to the boiling water absolutely transforms Batchelors Delicately Flavoured Rice, while to pour it liberally over Birds Eye Boil-in-the-bag Kipper Fillets elevates an already outstanding dish into food fit for a king. And what would Xmas dinner be like without it?

I wonder then why it is that TV chefs seem reluctant to use it. Could it be jealousy on their part, and that they don't like to admit that a healthy dollop of HP Sauce would improve even their finest efforts?

I would be interested in your comments.

Yours faithfully

T Ravenscroft (Mr)

HP Foods Limited

Our Ref:- GTH/JMJ/296

12 May

Mr T Ravenscroft
The Elms
Wenter Road
New Mills
High Peak
Derbyshire

Dear Mr Ravenscroft

Thankyou for your recent letter inquiring about using our product on National TV. I have passed your letter onto our Marketing Department for their comments and have been advised that it is very difficult to use branded products on TV programmes without contravening advertising regulations.

We do realise that products are used in demonstrations and in standard contracts, however, the presenter is under contract not to allow the brand name to be shown. These can be tailored to Company needs apparently. You never know we may be on the big screen soon!!

I do hope the above has clarified the situation for you but should you have any further queries please do not hesitate to contact us.

It is always pleasant to receive comments from valued customers, such as yourself, and we thank you for taking the time to write. From your letter you appear to thoroughly enjoy our products and use them in a variety of ways. Please find enclosed a product voucher to enable you to sample and enjoy some of our other brands such as Lea & Perrins Worcester Sauce, Amoy and Rajah with the same delight.

Yours sincerely

Jean James
Research and Development Administrator

The Elms
Wenter Road
New Mills
High Peak
Derbyshire

Jean James
HP Foods   15th May
Tower Road
Aston Cross
Birmingham
B6 5AB

Dear Jean James

Sorry, I appear to have made a mistake, it isn't HP Sauce I like, it's Heinz. However, with the voucher you kindly sent me I bought a bottle of your sauce, and whilst not reaching the heights which Heinz achieve, it is nonetheless very, very good, especially when a soupcon of it is added to a pot of Yorkshire Tea. If Heinz ever let their quality slip, which it appears they might well be doing if their Thomas The Tank Engine and Friends Pasta Shapes are anything to go by, I shall know where to turn. Thank you.

Yours sincerely

T Ravenscroft (Mr)

END OF CORRESPONDENCE

The Elms
Wenter Road
New Mills
High Peak
Derbyshire

English Provender Company
PO Box 5
Henley-on-Thames
Oxfordshire
R99 3PM

3rd May

Dear English Provender

My youngest son Oscar is extremely hyperactive, and short of tying him up the only way to stop him running riot is by strictly controlling his diet. However, this is only partially successful, and I am constantly on the lookout for additional means of slowing the little tyke down, short of amputation. It was with great expectations then that I tried him on your Provender Very Lazy Garlic. What a disappointment! Your product didn't make him any lazier at all, let alone very lazy. In fact, after I'd made him eat six slices of toast spread thickly with it, not only did it make him even more lively than usual, but he proceeded to scream the house down, and it couldn't have been the toast that was to blame because I'd made sure the bread I used was gluten-free.

I think I deserve an explanation of why your product is clearly failing to do what you claim that it does.

Yours faithfully

T Ravenscroft (Mr)

The Elms
Wenter Road
New Mills
High Peak
Derbyshire

Hovis Ltd
Claremont House
Yorkley
Nr Lydney
Glos

1st May

Dear Hovis

There are a number of Bovis homes under construction not far from where I live. As I passed by the other day, the bricklayers and their labourers were just starting their lunch break. I observed that each and every one of them was eating sandwiches made with Hovis bread. Now I realise of course that Hovis is popular, but ten men all eating it is too much of a coincidence, and I got to wondering if there is any connection between Hovis and Bovis, their names being so similar, and if the workers were getting subsidised bread. Could I be right? Is Bovis indeed a subsidiary of Hovis?

Incidentally, each of the workers was a fine figure of a man and a testament to your bread, with not so much an inch of buttock cleavage between them as far as I could discern.

Yours faithfully

T Ravenscroft (Mr)

KEARS GROUP LTD.

Claremont, Lydney, Glos. GL15 5DX

12th May

Mr T Ravenscroft
The Elms
Wenter Road
New Mills
High Peak
Derbyshire

Dear Mr. Ravenscroft,

Thankyou for your letter re Hovis bread and Bovis Homes, we would like to confirm that:

> THE TWO ARE NOT CONNECTED
> GOOD BREAD'S OUR CLAIM TO FAME
> BUILDING HOUSES JUST AREN'T US
> BRICKS JUST DON'T TASTE THE SAME
>
> THE REASON PEOPLE EAT IT
> BE THEY BUILDERS FIT OR NOT
> IS THE TASTE THE TEXTURE AND HEALTHINESS
> WITH HOVIS YOU GET THE LOT.

I hope this clears up your questions regarding Hovis Bread, but should you require any further information please do not hesitate to contact me.

Yours sincerely
KEARS GROUP LTD

L. CHILDS(MRS)
QUALITY ASSURANCE DEPARTMENT

The Elms
Wenter Road
New Mills
High Peak
Derbyshire

L Childs
Kears Group   19th May
Claremont House
Lydney
Glos
GL15 5DX

Dear L Childs

Thank you for your letter of 12th May. What an original and entertaining reply!

Since I wrote to you I have become quite friendly with the workers building the Bovis homes, and have discovered that most of them don't in fact eat Hovis bread, and what I took to be your bread was actually other brands of brown bread, notably Allinsons Stone Ground and Warburtons. It is ironic then that the only one of them who does eat Hovis, Declan his name is, is the least healthy-looking of the lot of them, having a definite humpback and a limp, although this could well be to do with him carrying a hod all day.

It would appear though that while Hovis may be trailing a little behind the others in its health-giving properties, it could very well make people poetic, because after I showed Declan your letter, he immediately offered the following ditty.

EAT BROWN BREAD
SHIT LIKE LEAD
NO BLOODY WONDER
FART LIKE THUNDER
EAT BROWN BREAD

I like to think of myself as a bit of a poet, but I am nowhere as adept at the art as your good self and Declan, so with this in mind, I am seriously considering changing to Hovis in the hope that it will improve my poems. I'll let you know if it does.

Yours sincerely

T Ravenscroft (Mr)

END OF CORRESPONDENCE

The Elms
Wenter Road
New Mills
High Peak
Derbyshire

St Ivel
Swindon   4th May
Wiltshire
SN4 8QE

Dear St Ivel

I have just had a couple of Hovis sandwiches made with your
Cheshire Cheese, and very nice they were too, with HP Sauce
and a few oven chips. When throwing away the wrapper, I
noticed that you make your Cheshire Cheese in Wiltshire. It's
none of my business of course, but wouldn't it be cheaper for
you to make the cheese in Cheshire, where the cows are?

Yours faithfully

T Ravenscroft (Mr)

St. Ivel Limited

ST. IVEL HOUSE
INTERFACE BUSINESS PARK
WOOTTON BASSETT   SWINDON
WILTSHIRE SN4 8QE

Mr T Ravenscroft
The Elms
Wenter Road
New Mills
High Peak
Derbyshire

GM/E/005/914/NH/SIWED
15th May

Dear Mr Ravenscroft

Thank you for your recent letter to St Ivel. We were very pleased to read your comments on St Ivel Cheshire Cheese.

With regards to your query about where we make the cheese, I would like to point out initially that all our cheeses are manufactured in Wales, and not in Wiltshire. In addition to this, the term "Cheshire Cheese" does not describe not the place where the milk (and therefore the cheese) is derived from, but the process which is used to make the cheese. In other words, Cheshire is a type of cheese, not the place where it is manufactured.

I hope this answers your query, and if I can be of any further assistance, then please do not hesitate to contact me.

Thank you for taking the trouble to write to us; I have enclosed a voucher which will help you to continue to enjoy St Ivel products in the future.

Yours sincerely

Miss Yael Bradbury
Customer Services Department

Enc Vouchers £1.00

The Elms
Wenter Road
New Mills
High Peak
Derbyshire

Yael Bradbury
St Ivel Ltd   19th May
St Ivel House
Interface Business Park
Wootton Bassett
Swindon
Wiltshire
SN4 8QE

Dear Yael Bradbury

I'm sorry, but your letter of 15th May has left me totally confused. You state that '… the term "Cheshire Cheese" does not describe not the place where the cheese is derived from'. I am familiar with the use of the double negative, so I am aware this means that Cheshire Cheese does describe the place from where the cheese is derived, i.e. Cheshire. This is confirmed by my Concise Oxford Dictionary, its entry reading 'Cheshire Cheese, originally made in Cheshire (county in England)'. However, you then go on to contradict yourself by saying that Cheshire is a type of cheese, not the place where it is manufactured, which is clearly at odds with what you have previously said, and also at odds with the Concise Oxford.

I am not happy about your cheese being made in Wales either, but I can see the logic of it as their singing probably turns the milk sour.

Yours sincerely

T Ravenscroft (Mr)

PS. I am intrigued by your Christian name. How did you come by it?

By Appointment to Her Majesty The Queen
Suppliers of Butter and Cheese
St. Ivel Ltd., Swindon, Wiltshire

St. Ivel Limited

ST. IVEL HOUSE
INTERFACE BUSINESS PARK
WOOTTON BASSETT SWINDON
WILTSHIRE SN4 8QE

Mr T Ravenscroft
The Elms
Wenter Road
New Mills
High Peak
Derbyshire

GM/E/006/074/KA/SIWED
20th June

Dear Mr Ravenscroft

Thank you for your letter of 19 May, commenting on our previous letter to yourself.

May we firstly point out that Miss Bradbury did not intentionally use a double negative; this was a careless mistake. The sentence was intended to read:-

> *the term "Cheshire Cheese" describes not the place where the cheese is made, but the process which is used to make the cheese.*

As to your reference to the Concise Oxford English Dictionary, may we draw your attention to the word "originally" in the sentence ("Cheshire Cheeese, originally made in Cheshire"). As we understand it, the process is determined solely on legal grounds. Some cheeses must be made in a particular place in order to gain the appropriate title, whereas others are permitted the title solely on the basis of the method of cheese-making.

We hope this has shed a little light on the matter, and not simply complicated it further.

Unfortunately, with regard to Miss Bradbury's Christian name, she was only here on a temporary contract and has since left the business and is therefore unable to help you further with its heritage.

Thank you once again for taking the time and trouble to contact us regarding our Cheshire Cheese.

Yours sincerely

Mrs G. A. Mitchell
<u>Consumers Services Department</u>

The Elms
Wenter Road
New Mills
High Peak
Derbyshire

Your ref
GM/006/074/KA/SIWED

30th June

Mrs G A Mitchell
St Ivel Ltd
St Ivel House
Interface Business Park
Wootton Bassett
Swindon
Wiltshire
SN4 8QE

Dear Mrs Mitchell

Thank you for your letter of 20th June, and for putting me right about 'Cheshire Cheese'.

With regard to Miss Bradbury, it wasn't necessary for you to use the euphemism 'left the business' to describe her departure – I am in business myself and am therefore well aware that one has to wield the axe occasionally. Notwithstanding this, however, I do feel that to dismiss her for making a careless typing mistake was a little harsh to say the least. With this in mind, and because I feel at least partly responsible for the poor girl's fate, I would be grateful if you could provide me with her address, as I wish to offer her a position in my Adult Calendars company.

Yours sincerely

T Ravenscroft (Mr)

The Elms
Wenter Road
New Mills
High Peak
Derbyshire

Pork Farms
55 Stallard Street
Trowbridge
Wiltshire
BA14 8HH

25th March

Dear Pork Farms

A couple of friends and I have just won a racehorse in a raffle.
We have to find a name for it and as we are all fans of your pies,
we thought we would call it Pork Farms Pork Pies. Have you any
objection to this? I don't think there's much chance of it ever
winning, as someone I know in the horseracing game says that
from the look of it if we entered it in the three o'clock race, there
would be no more than an outside chance of it being placed in
the three-thirty. However, I thought I'd better mention it in case
you feel that a horse called Pork Farms Pork Pies coming in last
might reflect badly on your pies.

Looking forward to hearing from you, with your blessing.

Yours faithfully

T Ravenscroft (Mr)

PORK FARMS BOWYERS

Queens Drive, Nottingham, East Midlands, NG2 1LU.

Mr T Ravenscroft
The Elms
Wenter Road
New Mills
High Peak
Derbyshire

Ref: Gj2011JJ   14 April

Dear Mr Ravenscroft,

Firstly, may I apologise for the delay in responding to your original letter, and secondly can I congratulate you on your recent good fortune. I must add that in my time at Pork Farms I have received some very unusual requests, but this is far and away the most unusual to date.

I am very pleased that both you and your friends are fans of our Pies, so much so that you would name your proud possession after them. However (and here is the boring legal bit), we cannot allow any use of the Pork Farms brand name outside of our corporate control. We would need to enter a licensing agreement that would need every aspect of your hobby being agreed to and signed off by our lawyers. I think you will agree that this would be a mutually tiring affair, particularly as the object of this exercise is fun. The more generic title of Pork Pie would, of course, be entirely down to yourselves.

I apologise for this slightly bureaucratic response, but we do need to ensure that the brand name is managed correctly. I will, however, look out for Pork Pie running in the 2.30 at Kempton and, despite your reservations about the horse's talents, have a small flutter.

Please find enclosed some vouchers that will hopefully please you all (even your equine friend)!!

Regards,

Gary Johnston

The Elms
Wenter Road
New Mills
High Peak
Derbyshire

Gary Johnston
Pork Farms Bowyers   25th April
Queens Drive
Nottingham
East Midlands
NG2 1LU

Dear Gary Johnston

Thank you for your letter of 14th April and the vouchers, although I really do wish you hadn't put the idea into my head of feeding your pork pies to our horse. The thing is, with the vouchers I bought eight pork pies, ate one of them myself – delicious, as usual – and fed the other seven to the horse. The following day, it dropped dead. The vet said it could very well have been the pork pies that caused the horse to go into the violent spasms that led to it having a heart attack, and that I was 'bloody stupid'. I must say his reasoning that eating seven pork pies can cause a heart attack is totally beyond me – I've eaten four of them many a time and the horse was twice as big as me, so if you ask me it is the vet who is bloody stupid. Anyway, I thought I'd better mention it to you so that you won't advise anybody else to feed pork pies to their racehorses.

On a more pleasurable note, having now owned a racehorse, my friends and I have really got the horseracing bug, so we're going to buy another one. I have checked with Tattersall's and it seems that there already is a horse called Pork Pies. (So great minds do think alike!) So we have decided to call our new horse Not As

Good As Pork Farm Pork Pies, which will fulfil the dual purpose of giving your firm a bit of a leg-up, whilst not using your brand name.

Would this be acceptable to you?

Yours sincerely

T Ravenscroft (Mr)

The Elms
Wenter Road
New Mills
High Peak
Derbyshire

Jordans
Consumer Care Team
Freepost BF 304
Biggleswade
SG18 9WE

21st February

Dear Jordans Porridge Oats

For the last three months, I have been breakfasting each morning on a bowl of your porridge oats as part of the GI (Glycaemic Index) diet, and very good they are too. They really fill me up and set me up for the day. This alone would make them well worth the price, but I have discovered to my great joy that your oats bring with them an added benefit, and a most welcome benefit at that!

I wouldn't like this to get around, of course, although I wouldn't object to you showing this letter around the office, but since starting to eat your oats, my sex life has improved no end. I suppose this is in part due to my being quite a lot slimmer and thus more attractive to my wife, having lost three stone since I started the diet (I am now down to a quite presentable nineteen stone), but I'm sure that my extra energy and staying power, fuelled as it is by your oats, has played an even bigger part.

I know from personal experience that regular helpings of milk-soaked anchovies can do wonders for a chap's sex drive, but I never suspected that porridge oats might do the same. Have any other of your customers experienced this phenomenon?

Yours faithfully

T Ravenscroft (Mr)

Mr T Ravenscroft
The Elms
Wenter Road
New Mills
High Peak
Derbyshire

5 March   Ref: 2007014580

Dear Mr Ravenscroft

Thank you for your very nice letter regarding our Conservation Grade Porridge Oats. It is so pleasant to receive your comments as we do try to maintain the highest standards of quality and value.

We do certainly listen to what our customers have to say and quite often changes in formulation take place because of popular opinion, although I don't think we will be putting your 'newly found extra benefit' down on pack as a unique selling point for our porridge oats but please be assured that I am passing copies of your letter over to our Technical and our Marketing Department, who always appreciate feedback from our customers especially when they are as positive as yours.

Thank you again for taking the time to contact us and for your support of Jordans.

Yours sincerely

Rita Farmer
Consumer Advisor

W. Jordan (Cereals) Limited, Holme Mills, Biggleswade, Bedfordshire SG18 9JY

The Elms
Wenter Road
New Mills
High Peak
Derbyshire

Rita Farmer
Consumer Advisor
8th March
W Jordan (Cereals) Limited
Holme Mills
Biggleswade
Bedfordshire
SG18 9JY

Dear Rita Farmer

Thank you for your prompt and courteous reply.

Despite what you say about not putting my 'newly found extra benefit' on your packet as a unique selling point for your porridge oats, I must say I think you are wasting a golden opportunity. However, I believe you may very well change your mind when you hear about the most wonderful slogan I have managed to come up with to promote your company's product. Wait for it … 'Get your oats with Jordans Oats.' Such a witty catchphrase is guaranteed to sell thousands of extra packets, I am quite sure. What do you think?

Unfortunately, I can't claim credit for the ditty as it was dreamed up by my friend Atkins Down The Road, who incidentally is now also a fan of your oats since I put him on to them a couple of weeks ago. Regarding Atkins, I must point out that, unlike me, he has not noticed any change in his sex life since breakfasting à la Jordans, but that isn't surprising as he claims to be a five-nights-a-week man even when oat-unaided, which isn't bad for a man in his early sixties, as I'm sure you will agree.

One further point. I notice you claim that your packets of oats may contain wheat, barley, rye, nuts, and sesame seeds. I must say, I'd never noticed any of these ingredients in your porridge, so I decided to investigate further. To my great surprise, and despite going through several packets with a fine toothcomb, I found not a single trace of any wheat, barley, rye, nuts, or sesame seeds. It is no business of mine of course, but I do feel that if you are claiming your oats contain any or all of these ingredients, you should make a greater effort to include them.

However, this is the only blot on an otherwise excellent copybook.

Yours sincerely

T Ravenscroft (Mr)

Mr T Ravenscroft
The Elms
Wenter Road
New Mills
High Peak
Derbyshire

14 March

Ref: 2007014580

Dear Mr Ravenscroft

Thank you for your recent letter regarding our
Conservation Grade Porridge Oats. Your slogan is very
good but if we put claims like you suggest on our porridge
oat packaging we will need to back them up with hard
facts and as you are the only customer who has informed
us of this precise benefit I don't think our legal department
will let us get away with it. If we have a customer who was
relying on this particular benefit and it did not happen for
him/her then we could be sued – with the litigation society
we live in these days.

The point you made about the "May contain" statement on
our packaging. This is yet another incident of our
marketing department thinking they are more open and
informative to our customers and all they have done is
cause confusion and distress to customers. The statement
is just to let customers who are severely allergic to these

allergens know that they are on our site as they go into products other than the specific product they have purchased.

I think your friend Atkins is quite a man, if his claims are true and if they can be proved to come with no artificial aids!!!!!!

Thank you for your letters and your support of Jordans.

Yours sincerely

Rita Farmer
<u>Consumer Advisor</u>

The Elms
Wenter Road
New Mills
High Peak
Derbyshire

Rita Farmer
Consumer Advisor   20th March
W Jordan (Cereals) Limited
Holme Mills
Biggleswade
Bedfordshire
SG18 9JY

Dear Rita Farmer

Thank you for your letter clearing up the 'May contain' business. I'm glad I'm not the only satisfied customer of Jordans that your Marketing Department has confused. Marketing people, eh? Almost as bad as social workers in my opinion.

Regarding my friend Atkins. I showed him your letter and he assured me that he has never used any artificial aids whatsoever, apart from the time his wife went to Australia for six weeks some years ago, when he sent away to a sex shop for a 'Wankey-Doodle-Dandy', which he used for five of the six weeks. It would have been six, but for some reason the contraption broke after five weeks, probably through overuse if I know Atkins.

Regarding my slogan. Yesterday afternoon I stationed myself in Tesco's breakfast cereal aisle for a couple of hours (I haven't much else to do, I'm retired) and asked every person who purchased a packet of your oats the following question: 'If you are following the GI Diet, has your sex life improved since you started eating Jordans Porridge Oats?' All of them answered my question, apart from two people who for some strange reason just looked at me with their mouths agape before wandering off, and a woman who slapped my face. Twelve of the hundred or so people I asked said they were on the GI Diet (8 women, 4 men). Seven of them (3 women, 4 men) thought that it had improved their sex life, 2 vastly. I would have stayed longer and questioned more of Tesco's very obliging customers, but unfortunately at that stage the manager asked me to move on, for some unknown reason.

It would seem then that you have a very strong case for including my slogan on your packet and in your advertising. Please feel free to do so. I took the names and addresses of the seven lucky people and if you would like me to pass them on to you so that they can confirm my findings, just say the word.

Yours sincerely

T Ravenscroft (Mr)

Nestle
Customer Services
PO Box 207
York
YO91 1XY

9th March

Dear Nescafe

Whilst I was on holiday in America recently, I came across Power Coffee, a beverage which contains 50 per cent extra caffeine. Naturally, I tried it, as I'm a man who can't get enough caffeine, being a real caffeine junkie, regularly drinking ten or more cups of coffee a day. I've heard it claimed by do-gooders that consuming a lot of caffeine isn't good for you, but it's never done me any harm. I can report that Power Coffee was quite wonderful; a cup of it not so much lifted me as picked me up, gave me a good shaking and inspired me to get out there and kick ass.

Now unfortunately I have a weak bladder and need the toilet a lot, which isn't always convenient as I am a long-distance lorry driver – or perhaps I should say I am a short-distance lorry driver who eventually drives a long distance, seeing as I have to keep stopping to go to the toilet, ha ha – but drinking Power Coffee when I was in America meant that I could drink only half as many cups of coffee for just as much caffeine, and consequently didn't have to go to the toilet as much. In fact, I only had to go once the whole five hours we spent in Disney World, whereas the previous time I went there I had to go four times, and one of those times was behind the Enchanted Castle as I couldn't find a toilet, which greatly embarrassed me.

Is it possible that you at Nescafe sell a version of Power Coffee? I am not hopeful as I've never seen it on the shelves at Tesco's and they sell just about everything, but there's no harm in asking, is there?

Yours faithfully

T Ravenscroft (Mr)

Nestlé UK Ltd

YORK YO91 1XY

Mr T Ravenscroft
The Elms
Wenter Road
New Mills
High Peak
Derbyshire

DATE

001874797A   14 March

Dear Mr Ravenscroft

Thank you for your recent letter.

Unfortunately Power Coffee is not available for sale in the United
Kingdom. Whilst sales do well in America, consumer research
suggests that demand in the UK would not be sufficient to justify
the long production runs necessary to ensure the good value
customers require.

Our experience with this and other brands leads us to conclude that
consumer tastes can vary considerably between different countries.
Nescafe Fine blend contains 4.6g of caffeine. Per 100g jar, 1
teaspoon is roughly 3g.

We hope this reply is not too disappointing. However, our marketing
policy is constantly under review and your comments have been
noted.

As I am sure you will appreciate, we receive many requests for information and we are not always able to go into great detail on the specific points raised. However, we enclose a booklet all about coffee which we hope you will find helpful.

Thank you once again for taking the trouble to contact us and for the interest you have shown in our Company.

Yours sincerely

Sue Tomlinson
Consumer Relations Executive
Consumer Services

The Elms
Wenter Road
New Mills
High Peak
Derbyshire

Sue Tomlinson
Consumer Relations Executive   17th March
Consumer Services
Nestle
PO Box 207
York
YO91 1XY

Dear Sue Tomlinson

Thank you for your letter. Shame that you don't do Power Coffee over here, but I'll survive, I suppose, it was just that the less I have to go to the toilet for a pee, the better I like it, as sometimes toilets aren't readily available.

However, I've had an idea. Do you think if I were to make a batch of your coffee, say a gallon, and boil it down to half a gallon, that it would double the caffeine content? Have a word with your boffins and let me know, would you?

Thank you also for the four wonderful booklets all about coffee which you sent, especially the one entitled *The Power of Love*, all about the Gold Blend couple Sharon and Tony. What a love story! I was an avid follower at the time, although I must say that my wife thought it was a bit soppy, but then that's about all you can expect from a lady wrestler.

I think you were wise not to mention that since drinking all that coffee Sharon died rather prematurely in *Holby City*. If you had done, some people might have thought it had something to do with your coffee, which I'm sure it wasn't, but you can't stop people talking, can you?

Looking forward to hearing from you.

Yours sincerely

T Ravenscroft (Mr)

Nestlé UK Ltd

YORK YO91 1XY

Register with Nestlé for the latest
product news & special offers
www.nestle.co.uk

Mr T Ravenscroft
The Elms
Wenter Road
New Mills
High Peak
Derbyshire

0018747978   21 March

Dear Mr Ravenscroft

Thank you for your recent letter concerning coffee.

With reference to your question, caffeine melts at 238 degrees centigrade.
It doesn't boil, but sublimes at 178 degs. So if you wanted to concentrate
some solubilised coffee to half its volume, the caffeine concentration would
approximately double as the temperature required to boil coffee mixture is
only just over 100 degs.

Thank you once again for taking the trouble to contact us and for the
interest you have shown in our Company.

Yours sincerely

Melanie Durkin
Consumer Relations Officer
Consumer Services

The Elms
Wenter Road
New Mills
High Peak
Derbyshire

Melanie Durkin
Consumer Relations Officer   29th March
Consumer Services
Nestle
PO Box 207
York
YO91 1XY

Dear Mel

Thanks for the very useful information. I wasted no time in making a batch of Power Coffee. At first I was going to boil two gallons of coffee down to one gallon to give me a beverage with 100 per cent added caffeine, but, never a man to go about things half-heartedly, I decided to distil the two gallons down to a bit under two pints, giving me a concoction which had a caffeine content of an extra 1,000 per cent.

What a brew! To try it out, I mixed a generous helping into our dog Rantzen's Pedigree Chum – I have nothing against experimenting on animals – and it didn't stop barking for two days. Then I tried it myself and realised what all the fuss was about.

I realise, of course, that caffeine stimulates the central nervous system, which is why I can't get enough of it, as I like to be stimulated, but I can honestly say that my central nervous system was stimulated beyond my wildest dreams. I drank just one mug full of it on Monday morning and I haven't been to bed since and today is Thursday. During that time, I have worked three shifts, driving over eight hundred miles (with no pit stops to go to the toilet, thanks to you), decorated our living room, dug the foundations for an extension, tarred the garage roof, twice run ten miles in training for the next London Marathon, made love four times and dug a dog's grave.

This stuff should be on prescription and I urge you to consider adding it to your range. It would be criminal not to.

Finally, I am looking for sponsors for when I take part in the London Marathon. All monies donated will go to good causes. Possibly towards a stone for Sharon of the Gold Blend ads if she hasn't already got one. Can I put you down for, say, a hundred pounds?

Yours sincerely

T Ravenscroft (Mr)

Nestlé UK Ltd

YORK YO91 1XY

Mr T Ravenscroft
The Elms
Wenter Road
New Mills
High Peak
Derbyshire

001874797C   12 April

Dear Mr Ravenscroft

Thank you for your recent enquiry.

As I am sure you appreciate, we receive many requests every year for financial or product donations. We were able to support over 20% of the fifteen thousand requests received last year and the total donated was £1,000,000. Although we would like to help everyone it is obviously not possible to do so.

We have considered your request for sponsorship very carefully but we are advised by our colleagues in Marketing that we are currently not able to offer support of this kind.

The aim of the Nestle Trust is to invest in partnerships and programmes which support the Nutrition, Health and Wellness of young people and which really make a positive difference to their lives. We tend to focus on local good causes which are well managed and relevant to the Company and where support will create goodwill within the community generally.

The key area for support is young people (specifically teenagers 11–18 year olds) in the following areas: Out of school childcare generally and specifically 4Children and Make Space, Nutrition, Health and Wellness, Sport, Education (but not areas which are Local Education Authority responsibility), Community Development.

Because of the number of requests we receive, we focus our support on charities or good causes which are local to our factories and depots, and, where appropriate, make a donation direct.

Thank you for taking the time and trouble to contact us and for giving us the opportunity to explain our position. I wish you every success in your fund-raising efforts.

Yours sincerely

Melanie Durkin
Consumer Relations Officer
Consumer Services

The Elms
Wenter Road
New Mills
High Peak
Derbyshire

Melanie Durkin
Consumer Relations Officer   24th April
Consumer Services
Nestle
PO Box 207
York
YO91 1XY

Dear Mel

Last Sunday, fuelled by Nescafe 1,000 per cent extra caffeine as recommended by your good self, I ran in the London Marathon. Sadly, you didn't feel able to sponsor me for this event, but I don't hold this against you, in fact quite the opposite, which is why I had the words 'Nescafe Made This Possible' emblazoned on my running singlet. Did you perhaps get a glimpse of me? I was running just behind a man pretending to be Rod Hull and Emu for a couple of miles (I wasn't chancing running in front of him after what he did to Michael Parkinson, even if this chap was only pretending!). I am told by friends that I was briefly on television three times, which is excellent publicity for Nescafe I am sure.

It was my hope of course to complete the course, but sadly this proved to be a little too much for me. However, I covered twelve and a half miles before I collapsed, which is almost halfway, and raised £433. In fact, I am fairly sure the TV cameras were on me when I lost consciousness. I am absolutely sure they were on me when a St John's Ambulance man revived me at the side of the road because the cameraman asked him to move to one side so he could get a good shot of me. You will be happy to know that even though I was still quite groggy, I had the presence of mind to point at the 'Nescafe Made This Possible' motto on my singlet.

In view of this, would you like to reconsider your decision not to sponsor me?

Yours sincerely

T Ravenscroft (Mr)

Nestlé UK Ltd

YORK YO91 1XY

Mr T Ravenscroft
The Elms
Wenter Road
New Mills
High Peak
Derbyshire

0018747970   1 May

Dear Mr Ravenscroft

Thank you for your recent letter.

Congratulations on your marvellous effort in the London Marathon and for
raising £433.00. We were sorry to learn that you failed to complete the
course and hope you have now fully recovered.

Further to our previous letter, in which we said we were unable to
sponsor you, there has been no change to the decision that we
communicated to you. Sorry if this response is disappointing for you.

Thank you once again for your interest in our products.

Yours sincerely

Gillian Liddell
Consumer Relations Officer
Consumer Services

END OF CORRESPONDENCE

The Elms
Wenter Road
New Mills
High Peak
Derbyshire

Spam
Tulip Ltd (UK)   31st March
Thetford
Norfolk
IP24 3SB

Dear Spam

About a month ago, I at last took the plunge, bought myself a computer and became a Silver Surfer. (Actually, I am a bald surfer, but I believe 'Silver Surfer' is the name that has been conferred upon old-age pensioner computer owners.)

With the computer and Internet connection came email, which I find very handy. One thing I don't find at all handy though is all the unsolicited email I am now receiving. Up to fifty messages a day and increasing daily. A younger friend who has been surfing for some time and has experience in these matters tells me that this unwanted mail is called Spam.

Which is the reason I am writing to you. Just what is your game? I can't for the life of me think why you should want to do this, except to make money. Why can't you people at Spam be satisfied doing what you are good at, i.e. making excellent chopped pork and ham luncheon meat, and stop sending people messages they don't want? The other day I had one asking me if I wanted to buy an inflatable rubber woman! Not only was this disgusting, but at £11.90 it was very poor value too.

Kindly remove my name from your mailing list at once.

Yours faithfully

T Ravenscroft (Mr)

SPAM up for the taste

Mr T Ravenscroft
The Elms
Wenter Road
New Mills
High Peak
Derbyshire

11 April

Dear Mr Ravenscroft,

Thank you for your letter of 31 March regarding Spam. We would like to assure you that we are not responsible for the SPAM mail you have been receiving via your email.

Spam mail is defined by the University of Glasgow as:-

> *"unsolicited, or "junk", email that is analogous to unwanted circulars that are received in paper mail."*

and is in no way linked with our company. If you wish to prevent unsolicited emails there are many different methods available on the internet to prevent such mail that can be found via an internet search.

Whilst you are on the internet you may wish to visit our site at www.spam-uk.com where you will find lots of real SPAM information, comments and recipes.

I hope this information is of use to you and would like to thank you for your interest in our brand.

Yours Sincerely

Stuart Neal
Technical Assistant

The Elms
Wenter Road
New Mills
High Peak
Derbyshire

Stuart Neal
Technical Assistant   14th April
Spam
Tulip Ltd (UK)
Thetford
Norfolk
IP24 3SB

Dear Stuart Neal

Ref your reply to my letter of 31 March.

Do I feel a fool! Thanks for putting me right. Thanks also for pointing me in the direction of your very interesting and informative website, on which I spent a pleasant half-hour or so this morning. I shall certainly be trying your Stinky French Garlic Spam, which sounds like heaven to a garlic lover like me. I shall have to purchase a can myself however, as my wife doesn't share my taste in garlic. She does however like regular Spam, which we have quite often.

In fact, your informing me of your website has solved a little problem I had vis-à-vis my other half. Her birthday is coming up very shortly and as usual I didn't know what to get her. I do now. A pair of your Spam Earrings, price £9.50. I have sent for a pair and can't wait to see her face when I give them to her.

Yours sincerely

T Ravenscroft (Mr)

The Elms
Wenter Road
New Mills
High Peak
Derbyshire

Stuart Neal
Technical Assistant
Spam   28th April
Tulip Ltd (UK)
Thetford
Norfolk
IP24 3SB

Dear Stuart Neal

Further to my letter of 14th April.

The Spam earrings arrived just in time for my wife's birthday, and very nice they were too. She said she liked them as much as she likes Spam, which is quite a lot, but thanks all the same but she didn't want them as she has several friends who are vegetarians and if she were to wear the Spam earrings in their company, it wouldn't be in very good taste.

I was therefore left with a pair of Spam earrings on my hands. However, so that they wouldn't be a complete waste of money, I decided to open them and have the Spam on a sandwich. Imagine my surprise when on opening up the little tins, I found them to be more or less solid metal with not a trace of Spam inside!

This is quite beyond the pale. I realise they are only earrings, but they are Spam earrings and as such should contain Spam in them. And now they can't even be used as earrings as I ruined them beyond repair trying to get the non-existent Spam out.

I would be interested in your observations.

Yours sincerely

T Ravenscroft (Mr)

The Elms
Wenter Road
New Mills
High Peak
Derbyshire

Hydes Brewery Ltd
46 Moss Lane West   17th March
Manchester
M15 5PH

Dear Hydes Brewery

I am writing to you in my official capacity as secretary of the New Mills Invalids Club. As part of our spring activities, the club would like to visit your brewery, if Hydes do a brewery tour, that is. If so, perhaps you could write to me stating prices, visiting times, discounts for invalids, et cetera.

I visualise that no more than twenty club members will be interested, as that is the number who took advantage of our trip to the Black Sheep Brewery in Yorkshire last year, which was most enjoyable apart from a couple of incidents.

One thing I must be aware of before our visit is if any of your overhead walkways are made of metal diamond mesh. I ask this because at the Black Sheep Brewery, one of our invalids, Mr Grimshaw, got his peg leg stuck in their overhead diamond mesh walkway, causing a half-hour delay and much embarrassment, especially when the tour behind caught up with us and couldn't get past. Why Mr Grimshaw insists on wearing a peg leg when proper artificial legs are freely available nowadays I really don't know, but I suspect it's because he likes people to know he was once in the Navy. Anyway, the thing is if Hydes have similar walkways, I shall simply tell Mr Grimshaw that he can't come.

You need have no fears however about the rest of we invalids. Despite our afflictions, we are all quite active, sound in mind if not in limb, and are able to get about (no wheelchairs) perfectly well. One of our two epileptic members caused us a bit of concern during the visit to Black Sheep when he had a fit and almost fell into a vat of fermenting hops, but you can rest assured that on our visit to Hydes I, as club secretary, will be keeping a very close watch on him.

Yours faithfully

T Ravenscroft (Mr)

THE MANCHESTER BREWER
— EST° 1863 —

HYDES BREWERY LIMITED
46 MOSS LANE WEST, MANCHESTER M15 5PH

Mr T Ravenscroft
The Elms
Wenter Road
New Mills
High Peak
Derbyshire

18th April

Dear Mr Ravenscroft,

With reference to your letter dated 17th March, firstly please accept my apologies for the delay in getting back to you.

We do operate tours at Hydes brewery that are available Monday to Thursday evenings throughout the year. The tours cost £7.50 per person which includes the tour of the brewery and a complimentary bar for the evening so you will be able to sample a wide selection of beers. However I do offer a discount for some groups and I would be happy to offer you places at £6.00 each. Tours start at 7:30pm and last orders is rung in the bar shortly before 10:00pm. You would need to arrange a date in advance so that I can reserve an appropriate number of places for you and the easiest way to do this is to give me a call and I will talk through the availability with you.

To the best of my knowledge none of our walkways are made of diamond mesh so there is little danger of Mr Grimshaw's peg leg causing any problems.

I look forward to speaking with you soon,

Kind regards,

Paul Mouat
Marketing Executive
Hydes Brewery

The Elms
Wenter Road
New Mills
High Peak
Derbyshire

Paul Mouat
Hydes Brewery Ltd   20th April
46 Moss Lane West
Manchester
M15 5PH

Dear Paul Mouat

You were so tardy in replying to my letter that I thought the prospect of your having to cope with Mr Grimshaw had put you off, but apparently I have misjudged you. Even so, I hope you are not so dilatory at Hydes in the manufacture of your ales or the pubs could soon run dry.

In fact, because you were so long in replying, I have in the meantime arranged a visit to Samuel Smith's Tadcaster Brewery in North Yorkshire instead. In addition to replying to my letter most promptly, they couldn't have been more helpful. One of their walkways is made of diamond mesh, but rather than say no to Mr Grimshaw, they have arranged to cover it with plywood during our visit, so as long as Mr Grimshaw's peg leg doesn't go through the plywood, everything will be hunky-dory.

I am still however interested in bringing a party of invalids to Hydes, but probably in the summer now. In view of the fact that you disappointed us with our proposed spring visit, would you be prepared to offer us a more generous group rate than £6.00 each? Say £4.00 each and £6.00 for the conjoined twins?

I look forward to your affirmative reply.

Yours sincerely

T Ravenscroft (Mr)

The Elms
Wenter Road
New Mills
High Peak
Derbyshire

Wm Morrison Supermarkets PLC
Hilmore House   9th March
Gain Lane
Bradford
BD3 7DL

Dear Morrison's

I am a sixty-eight-year-old man and I have been buying all the family's food from your supermarket for the last twenty years. Naturally, for a man of my years I am not as fit as I used to be. I don't want to bore you with my illnesses, and I don't really like talking about them, but if this letter is to fulfil its purpose, which I hope it will, I have little alternative.

In fact, I suffer from a hiatus hernia, a normal hernia (which thankfully I am going into hospital next month to have repaired), a trapped nerve in my spine which causes a little numbness in my arm, athlete's foot (just one foot), sciatica, arthritis, trouble with my prostate gland and anal pain.

The anal pain is by far the worst of my afflictions. I've tried everything to cure it, believe me. Conventional medicine, acupuncture, homeopathy, hypnotherapy, aromatherapy, all to no avail. I even tried, in absolute desperation, going to a faith healer, a travelling evangelist. At the meeting the evangelist laid hands on a man's lips and partially cured his stutter, then he laid hands on a woman's chronic bad back with an equally miraculous result, but when he laid hands on my bottom, he did nothing at all for it. I noted however that the evangelist didn't spend anything like so much time with his hands on my bottom as he had on the lips and back of the other two, so that maybe had something to do with it. I would have demanded my money back, but it was free, so I had to content myself with putting nothing in the collection box and taking a pound out to compensate me for the disappointment. But enough of my troubles.

The thing is, I've read a lot in the papers recently about the benefits of organic food – you are what you eat and all that – and having noted that you have now started stocking a large range of the same, I was wondering if you think it might benefit me health-wise if I switch from Morrison's normal food to Morrison's organic food. (Not of course that I in any way blame your food for my various complaints, in fact I got my hiatus hernia at Safeways when I used to shop there.)

Yours faithfully

T Ravenscroft (Mr)

Wm MORRISON SUPERMARKETS PLC

21st March

209/Ravenscroft/12311 lab

Mr T Ravenscroft
The Elms
Wenter Road
New Mills
High Peak
Derbyshire

Dear Mr Ravenscroft

Thank you for your letter to this department.

We always welcome feedback from our customers and assure you that your comments have been duly noted. I have taken the liberty of passing these onto the people concerned in order that this may be looked into and, if necessary, be addressed.

We pride ourselves on the high quality of products that we sell and it is always regrettable when these do not meet our customers' requirements. You can rest assured that your comments and views are very valuable to us and we will continue to do everything to ensure that we maintain the high standards that our customers expect.

Thank you once again for taking the time to share your views with us and I do hope that we will remain your choice for shopping in the future.

Yours sincerely
Morrisons Customer Services

Carol Paley
Customer Service Advisor

The Elms
Wenter Road
New Mills
High Peak
Derbyshire

Carol Paley   26th March
Customer Service Advisor
Wm Morrison Supermarkets PLC
Hilmore House
Gain Lane
Bradford
BD3 7DL

Dear Carol Paley

What's going on? I sent you the attached letter and you replied to it with what seems to be the standard reply to a letter of complaint. Kindly sort yourself out and reply to my original letter, would you?

Yours sincerely

T Ravenscroft (Mr)

Wm MORRISON SUPERMARKETS PLC

209/Ravenscroft/12311/JRW   13th April

Mr T Ravenscroft
The Elms
Wenter Road
New Mills
High Peak
Derbyshire

Dear Mr Ravenscroft

Thank you for your letter to this department. I am sorry that you are
disappointed with the response you have received in connection with
your complaint.

Our aim is to offer our shoppers outstanding value for money and we firmly
believe that all customers should have access to safe, wholesome,
affordable food, according to their individual tastes and preferences. We
believe we have a good range of organic foods, both own label and brands,
that includes bread, dairy products, eggs, fresh fruit and vegetables,
cereals, wine, tea and coffee and other grocery items, which we feel
reflects the current demands of the majority of our shoppers.

However, in relation to your question, I'm afraid that we are unable to offer
any advice if Organic food will help your medical condition. We would
advise that you seek advice from your GP.

Thank you once again for taking the time to bring this matter to our
attention and I do hope that we will remain your choice for shopping
in the future.

Yours sincerely
Morrisons Customer Services

Carol Paley
Customer Service Advisor

The Elms
Wenter Road
New Mills
High Peak
Derbyshire

Carol Paley
Wm Morrison's Supermarkets PLC   17th April
Hilmore House
Gain Lane
Bradford
West Yorkshire
BD3 7DL

Dear Carol Paley

You need have no fears that Morrison's will not remain my choice for shopping, not just in the future but for ever more! Why? Read on.

In the six weeks since I wrote to you, five of which I have been eating solely from your range of organic foods, my health has improved by leaps and bounds. While it is true to say that I haven't noticed any improvement with my bottom – in fact things have got a little worse in that department as I am breaking wind much more often than I used to, the organic broccoli probably – there has been a marked improvement in the state of my hiatus hernia, my sciatica and especially my athlete's foot, which has almost cleared up completely.

However, the best news is that my sex life has also improved, although this might have something to do with Jordans Porridge Oats, which are also organic of course. In fact, I am so delighted that I have had a T-shirt made with 'Morrison's Organic Food Is Simply Orgasmic' printed on the front (I am getting to be pretty nifty at slogan writing even if I say so myself).

On the only time I have worn the T-shirt at Morrison's thus far, it created quite a stir. Even the manager came out onto the shop floor to take a look at me, although it wasn't long before he was back in his office, but then he's a busy man, I suppose.

It was my intention just to wear the T-shirt when I am doing the weekly shop at Morrison's, but it occurred to me that I would be doing you a favour if I were also to wear it on the odd occasion I go to Tesco and Asda. In fact, if you like, as a small repayment for the huge debt I owe you, I would be quite happy to visit both of these supermarkets now and then and just walk around for a bit without buying anything, I don't think they can stop you. Would you like me to do this? It would be no trouble.

Yours sincerely

T Ravenscroft (Mr)

The Elms
Wenter Road
New Mills
High Peak
Derbyshire

Knorr
Freepost ADM 3940   23rd March
London
SW1A 1YR

Dear Knorr

I am afraid I have a complaint to make about your Ragu Tomato
and Cheese Sauce.

My wife was away for the day and I was busy, so I had our
Norwegian au pair Anni prepare a pasta dish for the children's
supper. To be quite honest, Anni's culinary skills are virtually
non-existent so I don't let her loose in the kitchen, only in
emergencies, and she doesn't speak very good English either,
however to make up for this she is very pretty and very
accommodating.

What happened apparently is that Anni followed the directions
on your packet a little too literally. Things went all right at first;
she tipped the contents of the pouch gently into a saucepan and
stirred often. It was when she carried out your serving suggestion
'for a tasty alternative throw in a small can of tuna and a
handful of peas' that things went pear-shaped. For that's what
Anni did, to the letter. She threw in a small can of tuna.
Unopened. She didn't get round to throwing in the handful of
peas because the force with which she threw in the tin of tuna
caused the saucepan to fly off the hob and deposit the Ragu
Cheese and Tomato Sauce on the floor.

I didn't witness the incident myself, but my eldest son Marcus
did. (Marcus was in the kitchen at the time because he likes

watching Anni. Well, he is fifteen now.) What my son said can be taken as gospel, because despite him wanting to be a solicitor when he grows up, I have yet to find him out in a lie.

The thing is that although your directions may be clear to all but the most stupid of English people, they are not at all clear to a not very bright Norwegian au pair who doesn't understand much English, and very probably not clear to many more not very bright foreigners too – I'm thinking here of the hordes of Poles and other East Europeans who have descended upon us recently – so with that in mind I think it might be prudent if you were to alter your directions from 'throw in a small can of tuna to 'throw in the contents of a small can of tuna'; or even better 'carefully add the contents of a small can of tuna', before a serious accident occurs.

Yours faithfully

T Ravenscroft (Mr)

Knorr Consumer Care
FREEPOST
250 Gunnersbury Avenue
LONDON
W4 5QB

Ref: 22918
Date   13 April

Mr T Ravenscroft
The Elms
Wenter Road
New Mills
High Peak
Derbyshire

Dear Mr. Ravenscroft

Thank you very much for your fabulous letter. I'm sorry to learn of your, or rather Anni's, recent experience with the Knorr Ragu For Kids pasta sauce. I can honestly say, this is the first time I have heard of this happening.

I'm sure you understand, when we propose an alternative serving suggestion we do intend that other products are fully removed from their packaging. We specifically use informal language on the pack to make the product more appealing to Kids and it seems as though the intended meaning got lost in translation. I have noted your comments and have forwarded them to the Knorr team for consideration.

I have also enclosed a voucher so you can purchase some more Ragu products. Hopefully these won't end up being assaulted by an unopened tin of tuna, and if they do, you can purchase spares with our compliments.

Unilever

Unilever UK Foods
a trading name of Unilever Bestfoods UK Limited
Registered in England & Wales No. 43520
Registered Office: Brooke House, Manor Royal,
Crawley, West Sussex, RH10 9RQ

Might I also suggest encouraging your son, Marcus, to adopt a more advisory role in the kitchen. It may stop other instructions being distorted by translation, and in turn will give him more time to spend with Anni.

Once again thank you for sharing your experience with us, and if you have any other queries or comments on any Unilever product then please do not hesitate to contact us again.

Yours sincerely

Amy Richmond
Careline Advisor

Enc.
Generic UF Coupon £5

Amy Richmond
Knorr Consumer Care   16th April
Freepost
250 Gunnersbury Avenue
London
W4 5QB

Dear Amy Richmond

Believe me, Amy, the state my son Marcus's hormones are in at the moment, the only advice he is likely to give to Anni is to get her knickers down, and as far as spending more time with her is concerned, it takes me all my time to keep the randy little bugger away from her as it is.

However, I must now return to the original incident in the kitchen involving your Ragu For Kids Tomato and Cheese pasta sauce. When the sauce was accidentally deposited on the floor, it left a stain on several of our cream vinyl tiles. At the time, I wasn't too concerned as I thought it would be a simple matter to remove it. How wrong I was, for despite trying everything I can think of, the stain has stubbornly refused to be removed.

My wife is not best pleased with me about this – I had to tell her that I was responsible for it as she had already threatened to send Anni back to Norway if she did anything else stupid, after the incident with the cat and the vacuum cleaner – so I was wondering if you can help to get me out of the doghouse by recommending something that will remove Ragu For Kids Tomato and Cheese pasta sauce stains? I notice from your letter that Knorr is part of the Unilever group, which, if my memory serves me correctly, sprang from the Lever Bros soap company, so as experts on getting things clean, you might be able to recommend something potent enough to do the job. And in view of the fact that you were in part responsible for the stain being there in the first place, perhaps you could send me a free sample? Or another £5 voucher would do, whatever you think best.

Yours sincerely

T Ravenscroft (Mr)

Knorr Consumer Care
FREEPOST
250 Gunnersbury Avenue
LONDON
W4 5QB

Ref: 22918
Date   25 April

Mr T Ravenscroft
The Elms
Wenter Road
New Mills
High Peak
Derbyshire

Dear Mr. Ravenscroft

Thank you once again for your letter with regards to Knorr Ragu For Kids, or now as the case may be the remnants of said product. I'm sorry to learn that this product left a mark on your kitchen and hope that this can be resolved.

We use all natural ingredients in the Knorr Ragu For Kids range so I can only assume that it is a rather stubborn tomato that refuses to leave the tiles in your kitchen. Once again I apologise for any inconvenience this may have caused, or indeed may be causing.

After talking to my good friends in the Home and Personal Care department, I can advise you try Cif Power Cream Spray which is specially designed for kitchen use. This should not only clear up the stain, but also clear your current 'doghouse' status.

Unilever UK Foods
a trading name of Unilever Bestfoods UK Limited
Registered in England & Wales No. 43520
Registered Office: Brooke House, Manor Royal,
Crawley, West Sussex, RH10 9RQ

If you have any other queries with regards to Unilever products or require further advice on this issue, please do not hesitate to contact us at the above address. Please find enclosed a voucher to enable you to try Cif with our compliments.

Yours sincerely

Amy Richmond
Careline Advisor

Enc.
277 HPC Coupon £5

The Elms
Wenter Road
New Mills
High Peak
Derbyshire

Amy Richmond
Knorr Consumer Care
Freepost
250 Gunnersbury Avenue
London
W4 5QB

1st May

Dear Amy

I must say that Knorr is the most generous company I have ever dealt with, and I have dealt with a few. Twice I have written to you and on each occasion not only have you had the courtesy to write back to me promptly and efficiently, but you have enclosed a voucher for £5. The only way this could have been bettered would have been if you had sent me £5 in cash, because to tell you the truth I don't buy Unilever products all that often (mind you, I may not be familiar with them all, so maybe you can send me a complete list?). My wife says you are trying to bribe me so that I won't start blabbing about your pasta sauce ruining our kitchen tiles, but I prefer to think you are a caring company, like Baxters Soup, who sent me a shedload of vouchers when I had cause to complain about their Cock-a-Leekie soup, and even as I write are considering my recipe for Cock-of-Puddings.

I tried your Cif Power Cream Spray as recommended by your good friends in the Home and Personal Care department, as you suggested, and it almost got rid of the stain. I say almost, in fact to my eyes the stain has disappeared altogether, but my wife swears she can still see something and she could be right because the woman has eyes a hawk would be proud of, believe me. Anyway, I've moved the pedal bin over the alleged stain so it should no longer be a problem.

Yours sincerely

T Ravenscroft (Mr)

Ref: 22918
Date   11 May

Mr T Ravenscroft
The Elms
Wenter Road
New Mills
High Peak
Derbyshire

Dear Mr. Ravenscroft

Thank you once again for your letter. I'm glad to hear that the Cif Power Cream Spray worked, at least a little!

I'm sorry to learn that your wife thinks we are bribing you with vouchers, and can assure you that this is not the case. We merely want to rectify any issues, and address any comments you have or may have had with Unilever products. It is after all, what we are here for.

The following is a list of Unilever products available in the UK. Adez, Bertolli, Boursin, Bovril, Colman's, Elmlea, Flora, Flora Omega 3 Plus, Flora Pro.activ, Hellmann's, I Can't Believe It's Not Butter, Jif, Knorr, Lipton Ice Tea, Marmite, Peperami, PG Tips, Pot Noodle, Scottish Blend, Slim Fast, Stork, Summer County, Carte D'Or, Cornetto, Magnum, Solero, Wall's and Viennetta, Brut, Dove,

Unilever UK Foods
a trading name of Unilever Bestfoods UK Limited
Registered in England & Wales No. 43520
Registered Office: Brooke House, Manor Royal,
Crawley, West Sussex, RH10 9RQ

Impulse, Lux, Lynx, Mentadent, Pond's, Signal, Sunsilk, Sure, Timotei and Vaseline, Cif, Domestos and Persil.

You could also visit our website for more information. It has cleverly been called www.unilever.co.uk. The individual brands also have their own websites with more information about specific ranges.

I'm aware that another voucher to try one of our products may be inappropriate. As a thank you for contacting us, I have taken the liberty of including an eclectic mix of Unilever items. I hope you enjoy these, and look forward to any comments you may have.

Yours sincerely

Amy Richmond
Careline Advisor

Enc.
34 Colman's product range
108 Hellmann's 'Your Sandwich Made It!' book
128 Marmite – Set of Beer Mats
114 ICBINB! Halloween Face Paint Pack

The Elms
Wenter Road
New Mills
High Peak
Derbyshire

Amy Richmond
Knorr Consumer Care   18th May
Freepost
250 Gunnersbury Avenue
London
W4 5QB

Dear Amy

Thank you for the gifts, which far from allaying my wife's suspicions that you are bribing me have only served to increase them. But then she is a suspicious woman as I have sometimes found to my cost, and it is only a matter of time before she makes good her threat to send Anni back to Norway.

With the vouchers you have sent thus far I purchased another Cif Power Cream Spray (in the hope that it would work better than the previous one; it didn't, so the pedal bin will have to remain where it is for the time being), a packet of I Can't Believe It's Not Butter (I can, by the way, and can't believe why anybody can't), a packet of Boursin, a jar of Marmite, a jar of Hellmann's Mayonnaise, two packets of Peperami, a sachet of Slim Fast and a jar of Vaseline. I then sliced a baguette in half, spread the I Can't Believe It's Not Butter on it, thought better of it, scraped it off and spread Lurpak butter on it, then piled on the Peperami, all the Boursin, the sachet of Slim Fast, half the Marmite, two generous dollops of the Hellmann's Mayonnaise and a teaspoonful of Vaseline.

My idea is that although this very tasty sandwich contains a host of fattening foods, they will be neutralized by the Slim Fast, giving a sandwich that is not only extremely tasty, but also non-fattening. (You might question the inclusion of Vaseline, but apart from adding a certain something to a sandwich, it helps it to slip down, and is a must with bacon or sausage.)

I intend to enter this sandwich for your next 'Your Sandwich Made It!' book. It feels like a winner to me.

Yours sincerely

T Ravenscroft (Mr)

END OF CORRESPONDENCE